T0196982

LIFE BRINGS
HARD CHOICES
SOMETIMES YOU JUST HAVE TO
RUN OVER THE SKUNK

PATRICIA ALEXANDER OWENS

WESTBOW
PRESS®
A DIVISION OF THOMAS NELSON
& ZONDERVAN

Copyright © 2023 Patricia Alexander Owens.

All rights reserved. No part of this book may be used or reproduced by any means, graphic, electronic, or mechanical, including photocopying, recording, taping or by any information storage retrieval system without the written permission of the author except in the case of brief quotations embodied in critical articles and reviews.

WestBow Press books may be ordered through booksellers or by contacting:

WestBow Press
A Division of Thomas Nelson & Zondervan
1663 Liberty Drive
Bloomington, IN 47403
www.westbowpress.com
844-714-3454

Because of the dynamic nature of the Internet, any web addresses or links contained in this book may have changed since publication and may no longer be valid. The views expressed in this work are solely those of the author and do not necessarily reflect the views of the publisher, and the publisher hereby disclaims any responsibility for them.

Any people depicted in stock imagery provided by Getty Images are models, and such images are being used for illustrative purposes only.
Certain stock imagery © Getty Images.

Scripture quotations marked KJV are from the Holy Bible, King James Version (Authorized Version). First published in 1611. Quoted from the KJV Classic Reference Bible, Copyright © 1983 by The Zondervan Corporation.

Scripture quotations marked NIV are taken from the Holy Bible, New International Version®, NIV®.
Copyright © 1973, 1978, 1984 by Biblica, Inc.™
Used by permission of Zondervan. All rights reserved worldwide.

Scripture quotations marked NLT are taken from the Holy Bible, New Living Translation, copyright © 1996, 2004, 2007 by Tyndale House Foundation. Used by permission of Tyndale House Publishers, Inc., Carol Stream, Illinois 60188. All rights reserved.

ISBN: 978-1-6642-9427-1 (sc)
ISBN: 978-1-6642-9425-7 (hc)
ISBN: 978-1-6642-9426-4 (e)

Library of Congress Control Number: 2023904111

Print information available on the last page.

WestBow Press rev. date: 03/21/2023

WITH LOVE

To my three sons, my grandchildren, and my great grandchildren

Now that I am old and gray, do not abandon me, O God.
Let me proclaim your power to this new generation,
your mighty miracles to all who come after me.
—Psalms 71:18 NLT

CONTENTS

PREFACE

Driving along a narrow, twisty country road, I rounded a curve, popped over a hill, and immediately saw a skunk in the middle of the road.

Just minutes before, I had received a frantic phone call and had hurriedly left my house and was on my way to try to provide help to a beloved family member. I found myself driving as fast as safely possible to get there, when the skunk suddenly appeared. For obvious reasons, I didn't want to hit the skunk, but I thought I might have to hit it anyway. Thankfully, I was able to avoid the skunk, but all of a sudden, it dawned on me!

Sometimes, there *are* no good choices!

Sometimes, you just have to *run over* the skunk!

That thought stuck with me!

In the next few weeks, while continuing to be concerned about current family problems, trying to provide counsel and advice, and discussing various options and choices with my family members, I found myself thinking about my life of almost eighty years and some of the choices I had made over the years.

Throughout my life, I had been faced with many *hard* decisions and choices, some of which were now being contemplated by my own children and grandchildren. Some of the choices were of my own choosing, and some were forced upon me by other circumstances.

With some of the choices, I had time to weigh the consequences.

Other decisions had to be made almost instantaneously. Some were very inconsequential. Other choices were monumental and were very difficult to make. Some I really did not want to make at all, as they were life-changing, and they often resulted in unpleasant circumstances. Many times throughout my life, when there seemed to be no good choice, I had to figuratively run over the skunk, and I knew my children and grandchildren—as well as many others—would have their own difficult choices to make as well.

At times in my life when I did, in fact, have to run over the skunk, I often had to spend a lot of time afterward trying to get rid of the stink. Sometimes, with a little work, help, or with some "deodorizing," I found I actually *could* get rid of the stink, or the stink would dissipate, and I could go on as usual with a somewhat normal life.

Sometimes, it took weeks, months, or even years of trying to get the stink to go away. On other occasions, after trying so hard and working so long at trying to get rid of the stink, or when the smell was so deeply embedded and unyielding, I had an even harder choice to make. It was on those occasions when I sadly decided that I just needed something *new* or *different*, or at least, I needed to go in a *different direction*.

Twenty years ago was a turning point in my life when I had one of those difficult decisions to make. I felt I needed to be going in a different direction. It was a time when I had to run over the skunk!

INTRODUCTION

I was sitting alone, silently staring out the window at the Chili's restaurant in Lexington, Kentucky, when I suddenly thought to myself:

> This isn't the way my life was supposed to turn out! This shouldn't be happening to me! This is not what I wanted for my life! I am retired now! I am almost sixty years old! I am supposed to have my life altogether! At this age and stage in life, I am supposed to be able to give my children and grandchildren good advice and be a good example to them, but just look at me ... I still need advice and help myself!

It was about 3:00 p.m., and I was having a late lunch. The restaurant was virtually deserted as it was midafternoon, halfway between the regular business lunchtime crowd and the early dinner crowd. Anticipating my *third divorce*, I was in a very pensive mood as I had just finished one of many sessions with my marriage counselor and was getting ready to go to a financial meeting with my lawyer.

This wasn't at all how the stories ended in the modern romance comic books I had read when I was in high school. I was supposed to fall in love, get married once and forever, have a wonderful husband, have perfect kids, and live happily ever after. But here I was, just a little farm girl from Big Clifty, Kentucky, contemplating a divorce for the *third* time. I had never dreamed or imagined that I would ever be in that position for the *first* time, let alone for the *third* time.

After five years of ups and downs, ins and outs, back and forth, moving out and coming back, good days and bad days, my third husband and I were on the verge of a divorce. I wanted to save our marriage. I didn't want to fail a third time!

We had tried five different counselors, but each time, after a few sessions, I was the only one who wanted to continue with the weekly sessions. With the last counselor, I continued on my own for over a year. The counselor did not promise me he could save my marriage, but he *did* promise that, if I continued with counseling sessions long enough, my life would get better. And it *did* start to get better!

My present marriage was not what I then believed and understood a godly, Christian marriage relationship to be. My husband and I had gone back and forth for five years, with no mutual commitment to make our marriage better or to save our marriage. Without that mutual commitment to change and the decision to work together, I felt that the relationship between my third husband and me was doomed to fail.

After waffling back and forth for five years, some difficult choices needed to be made. To me, there were *no good choices*! I realized that *not* making a choice, and continuing to drift along with no joint commitment, would actually be a choice in itself. I knew that whatever choice I made or didn't make, there would be unpleasant consequences for me to face.

That was a time when I just had to run over the skunk!

So I did!

I decided to start anew! Now I had to try to get rid of the stink! I had to begin to deal with all the unpleasant consequences.

As a result of my decision, there *were* indeed many unpleasant consequences. As with any unwanted breakup, I was experiencing the heartache and sadness that many others also experience. I was alone again. I had suffered the embarrassment of another failed marriage. I felt added guilt based on my religious beliefs. I lost joint friendships that my husband and I had once enjoyed together. I lost a relationship with his family that I had enjoyed.

Living in a household with one income, I had to learn to better manage my finances. I became responsible for everything—from housework, household upkeep and repairs, and yard work, to concern for my own health and safety. I was alone for social events and at family gatherings.

Most regrettable to me was knowing that my children and grandchildren had been deprived of the godly example of two parents and grandparents sticking together through thick and thin, for better or worse, and enjoying loving family time together with them in our old age.

That choice of a third divorce—difficult though it was for many reasons—and the years of healing that came afterward, helped me to realize that with time, help, and especially with God in my life, there *is* hope for renewal, it *is* possible to get rid of the stink, and happiness and peace *can* come after three divorces and much sorrow and regret. That choice made twenty years ago began a different, satisfying, and peaceful phase of my life.

Some of the earlier years of my life could be likened to a soap opera, and in many respects, that would be true. This book is *not* meant to share all those salacious details. I do not want to besmirch or minimize the feelings of any person who might have been part of my soap opera years. Each of them has his own story to tell and his own responsibilities to bear.

I want to note just enough information about some of my specific relationships, experiences, and choices to enable me to relate some of my *own* personal feelings, thoughts, or responses to them, and how they helped to shape my life. I want to share some of my personal upbringing and history, and focus on looking inward as to my responsibility for decisions I made both as a child and as an adult. As part of my story, I want to note some of the lessons I have learned throughout my eighty years. Many of my thoughts and beliefs have been refined *because of* or *in spite of* these different relationships, experiences, and choices.

Most of my memories, experiences, and choices are centered around farm life, children, family, education, and religion. Other readers may share similar commonalities. If you identify with any of the following, you may find this book interesting to read:

- If you love farm life and country living, and grew up with few luxuries
- If you love children and enjoy their humor and antics
- If family is important to you
- If you are a parent, grandparent, or great-grandparent
- If you are a teacher or an educator
- If divorce is a part of your history
- If you have ever struggled with your religious beliefs
- If you have been faced with difficult choices in your life

Throughout relating my personal memories, I want to summarize and share some of the most memorable ones, beginning with those in my earliest years. I could write an entire book about some of the individual experiences I have featured in some of the chapters, but I cannot possibly include details of all the memories and interactions of each in just one book. Each step along the way brought both growth and learning in my life's journey, whether when I was living at home with my parents or later in life after I left my parents' home.

Many of my memories include strong spiritual elements, which are interwoven throughout my lifelong experiences. Over time, these embedded truths helped me to grow, learn, and change. They helped me to overcome some difficult circumstances, while at the same time creating more awareness and gratitude for my many blessings.

Some readers may identify with experiences I have had or choices I have made, those which they themselves have faced or *will* face. Just as *my* choices and experiences have helped shape my life and have led me to be the person I am today, the same will be true for each of them. They will undoubtedly make mistakes, experience failures, and face difficult choices of their own. There will be times when, faced with a difficult decision, they, too, may find that they might have to run over the skunk.

At those times, I want them to know, as I have learned, that there is always hope for a new beginning.

God's mercies are new every morning!
—Lamentations 3: 22-23 KJV

As I near the end of my life, I'm very thankful that I now have that long sought-after inner peace and joy. I wish that same blessing for my beloved children, grandchildren, great-grandchildren, my extended family, my friends, and any other reader. With God in their lives, I pray that each of them will find that inner peace and joy—*just as I did*!

O N E

Earliest Memories

Choices, whether wise or unwise, always have consequences which are either pleasant or unpleasant.

One choice we do *not* have is the family into which we are born!

For most children, choices are made for them by their parents when the child is in their early years, and even up to the time when they leave home and are on their own. At least that was my experience. As long as my brothers and sisters and I were living at home with our parents, and they were providing a living for us, we had to follow their rules. In our house, there was usually only *one* choice, which was to *obey our parents* or suffer the consequences. Daddy had the final say-so! At times, when we made unacceptable choices, we often suffered the consequences of a peach tree limb or a belt, and that was a fairly good deterrent for misbehavior or complaining.

As young children, in our family, we were not involved in the decision-making process as to where we wanted to live, where we might want to move, what we wanted to eat, where we wanted to go for dinner, what kind of clothes we had to wear, whether or not we wanted to help with chores, or many other choices that seem to be given to many children today. About the only decisions we made at our young ages were whether or not we wanted to obey our parents, to do what we were told, or to suffer the consequences. That pretty much continued throughout my school years and until I grew up and left home.

Ephesians 6:1 NIV was a known and often quoted scripture, and it was the abiding rule in our house as I was growing up.

1

"Children obey your parents in the Lord, for this is right."

One of my earliest childhood memories was living beside the railroad tracks in Big Clifty, Kentucky. I can remember two elderly next-door neighbors who were always kind to us, and another neighbor who lived just down the road. Our yard was right next to the switch track, where a train stopped to let another train pass. At that time, in the 1940s, as very young children, we would almost daily stand out in our yard and wait for the train. In those days, there was always a red caboose at the end of the train, and we anxiously waited for it to stop near our yard and house on the side track. We were patiently waiting to see the man in the red caboose, who would be sitting up high in the caboose and looking out the window. We were waiting for him to talk to us or wave to us, but mainly, we were waiting for him to give us bananas, which he usually did. Bananas were a real treat to us when we were very young children, as this was a difficult time for families such as ours during the war years.

Though we didn't realize it in those younger years, this was perhaps the beginning of some of the values my siblings and I observed and learned that carried over into adulthood. From our observations and experiences in childhood, we were beginning to form values during our formative years. Even at this early age, through this one interaction of getting a banana, we experienced kindness and generosity from the man in the caboose, who was a complete stranger.

Another distinct memory I have at that house by the tracks was when my older brother drank some kerosene. Mama grabbed him and, with the rest of us kids tagging behind, ran over to the neighbor's house, which was just down the road. Mama was upset, and I remember the neighbor lady putting my brother (who wasn't much older than me) in a high chair in her kitchen and giving him some milk to drink. This would supposedly dilute the kerosene and lessen its effects. On that day, we witnessed examples of friendship, neighborliness, caring, and helpfulness.

We soon moved from that house beside the tracks to an old log house on a farm in Big Clifty, Kentucky, and lived there while our new, big house on the hill was being built. I was three years old when we moved into the old, two-story log house. The floor of that old log house sagged in the middle. There was a big potbellied stove in the middle of the front room.

One memory I have that stands out from while we were living there was when the house caught on fire. I remember seeing Granny Duvall (God rest her soul) hurriedly coming down the steep stairs, trying to get away from the smoke. Even though it is now long gone, the old house actually survived at the time, and thankfully, none of us were harmed.

While living there, I remember Daddy throwing a pack of cigarettes into the roaring fire in the big potbellied stove, announcing to us all that he was going to quit smoking. And he did! After that day, I never saw him smoke again. He kept chewing gum in his pocket after that, probably to help him kick the habit. This proved to be a plus for all us kids, as quite often the chewing gum became a treat to us when Daddy might give us a stick of his favorite Juicy Fruit gum. These experiences, whether or not I knew it at the time, were examples of self-discipline, courage, and responsibility. Our parents were teaching by example.

Daddy was a rural mail carrier, and at one time, he had a car with a running board. We could see him coming home from work down that old dirt road to our log cabin. We were always glad to see him, and we little kids would run out to meet him. It didn't matter that the road was often muddy with deep ruts. He would let us get up on the running board, hold onto the side of his car, and ride up to the house with him as he watched and slowly drove and parked in the grass next to the house. Letting us ride like that would probably be seen as child endangerment in today's world, but to us, these were memorable and pleasurable experiences. We were learning that we could be happy with the little everyday pleasures of life that cost nothing but a little thought and kindness from our daddy.

I remember our family taking only one trip while we lived in the old log house. We went to Neponset, Illinois, to see one of Mama's sisters. We went in the breezy old Jeep, which Daddy had at the time for carrying mail on his rural mail route. I rode in the back and sat on one of the hard side seats. It was so very cold on the way, as the sides of the Jeep were continually flapping in the cold air as we drove along. In spite of that, I thought the trip was special. At least we got to go somewhere, and most special to me was when we stopped along the way, and I was treated with a Nehi orange drink. That may not seem like much today, but treats like that were not enjoyed by children in our family very often. The virtues of gratitude and appreciation were being formed.

Even before the house was completely finished, we moved into our new home on the hill at the family farm. We moved in when I was four years old. We walked up planks leading through the front door, as no steps had been built at that time. Grandpa and Grandma Hawkins moved in with us for a while until their house across the road on Highway 62 was ready for them. Granny Duvall also moved with us into the new house. She had her own room upstairs and was still living in that house when I got married and moved out. These choices and experiences were examples of respect and honor for parents, generosity, flexibility, patience, and living within our means.

This big two-story house in Big Clifty became the home place, where all six of us children grew up, and where my brother and sister-in-law still live today. My youngest sister was born there. I remember that day. A lady across the road came to help the doctor. The rest of us kids were sent outside to play. I remember standing outside near Mama's bedroom window, trying to hear what was happening. It was very scary for me, as I could hear Mama moaning and groaning as she cried out in pain while she gave birth there in her bedroom.

When we first moved into our new home place, there was still a lot of work to do on the house. It was livable, but there were several things that had not yet been completed. Initially, we had no indoor bathrooms. Instead, we had an outhouse not too far from the back door. I used to joke that we were rich, because our outhouse was a two-seater, even though I don't remember two of us ever being in it together and using it at the same time.

There was always lime in the outhouse, which might serve the same purpose as air fresheners today. Between the seats in the outhouse was the Sears, Roebuck and Co. catalog, which served the same purpose as our toilet tissue today. I could spend a lot of time looking through those catalog pages while sitting in the outhouse, thinking of things I liked or might wish I had. The catalog was luxurious toilet tissue compared to the use of leaves and corncobs, which were used when we were out all day in the woods or working in the barn. (Yes, really!) After dark, it was a little better, as we had "pots" in our rooms to use if we needed to go to the bathroom during the night. Of course, in the morning, the pots had to be emptied and cleaned. I still have one of those pots in my garage today, after all those years—just in case!

When it could be afforded, two bathrooms were added to our house, one upstairs and one downstairs. Until then, with very little complaining or discussion, we adapted and learned to be content with our circumstances at the time. Our parents were making these choices for us as we were very young children.

Be grateful and happy with what you have while working for what you want!

This maxim definitely applied to our family situation and circumstances during those early months of moving into the house on the hill.

TWO

Full House with Granny

Our big new house was a full house! Living in the home place on the hill, there were six of us—four girls and two boys. In the order of birth were Victor, Patsy, Brenda, Jane, Ben, and Mary Ann, all of us born within a ten-year period. Also living there were Mama, Daddy, Granny Duvall, and Grandma and Grandpa Hawkins. Grandma and Grandpa Hawkins only lived there for a short time until their new house across the road was finished. Granny Duvall lived with us in that house from the time we moved there until I got married and moved out. She actually lived there for many years thereafter—basically, for the rest of her life.

Everyone in our house knew who was in charge. All of us respected that, even Mama and Granny Duvall. None of us as young kids ever questioned or argued with Daddy about anything. We had a very healthy respect for his parental authority. For most of our time at home, we never even thought to disagree with his decisions. As we grew older and were becoming more independent, there were some normal disagreements. Sometimes, these involved Daddy wanting to hold on and be protective of his children, or my siblings and I beginning to want to make more of our own decisions and to spread our wings.

For all of my years at home, Granny Duvall had her own areas of responsibility and was always doing something to help the family.

I don't remember Granny ever talking about Grandpa Duvall. I don't remember ever seeing him myself. From stories I heard, he had an alcohol problem, and even though Granny Duvall did not live with him, she never divorced him. She always lived with us—Mama, Daddy, and her six grandkids—until shortly before she died. Our home became her home.

When I was younger and was still living at home, I sometimes thought Daddy was mistreating Granny. If he saw that she might be disagreeing with Mama about some household decision, or that she was trying to have the last word, he would say something to her like, "Now, Mother, you just need to let Gladys handle that!" or, "Gladys is running this household!" or, "Mother, you might just need to go to your room!"

To me, as a young person, that sounded harsh, but as I grew older and had a family of my own, I completely understood why it had to be that way, and even later, I got to tell Daddy how my thoughts had changed. It was quite a loving sacrifice for him to take care of his mother all those years, and it was a loving sacrifice as well for Mama to have her mother-in-law living with her for so many years. Even with much love among them all, if Granny was to live in the same household with her daughter-in-law, Daddy had to put Mama first, and Granny had to know that.

In our later discussions, Mama acknowledged what a help it had been to have Granny living with us all those years, and the valuable contributions she had made to our family and us six children, and how much she loved Granny and cared for her. Raising six children, all so close together in age, understandably required a lot of time, energy, and effort, and having Granny Duvall there was definitely a big help. She was an integral part of our family.

Granny was pretty much in charge of the flower garden on the home place. She had beautiful flowers and spent many hours hoeing, spraying, weeding, and pruning to keep the flower garden looking good. Often, some of us would go out and work with her. On any day, if we wanted to, we could cut flowers and bring them inside. There was always something pretty blooming all throughout the year, and whenever we wanted, we could have beautiful fresh flowers on the table or in our rooms to enjoy or to give to others.

I think that was just one of the things that contributed to everyone in our family learning to appreciate the beauty of nature. Granny's love of flowers was shared by Mama, and as a result, was passed on notably to me and my siblings, with all of us loving and having beautiful flowers and gardens at various times throughout our lives.

We have *all* shared a love of flowers, gardening, and nature—some of us more extensively and passionately than others. We have even been able to share with our own children and their families some starts from flowers in the flower garden that Granny had helped to tend at the old home place. Many of the plantings are also still being enjoyed by Ben and Wanda, my brother and sister-in-law, who continue to live there on the old family farm.

One of Granny's major contributions to our family was as a seamstress. She was an excellent seamstress! She did professional work, and she could make anything! When we were growing up, she made most of our clothes, including dresses and coats. She could turn old, worn-out things into items of clothing we could wear, which was very valuable to our family in our early years. Today, a sock with a hole in it would more than likely be thrown away, but Granny would have fixed it. She would put a light bulb into the heel of the sock, and she would proceed to darn the sock, stitching back and forth over the light bulb, to make it wearable again. Her reconstructive work on many items was amazing!

For the girls, Granny made dresses from feed sacks. We took turns getting a dress made by her. When the feed was delivered for the animals, there was always more than one bag with the same pattern, and after the bags were emptied and washed, Granny would start on a dress for one of us. If it was our turn to get a new dress, we were always anxious to see the bag in which the feed had been delivered. We could then visualize our new dress as Granny started with the pattern, the sewing, and the fitting, until we finally got to wear the finished outfit made by her.

I didn't have a store-bought dress until I was a junior in high school. That was the most beautiful dress in the world to me. It was a light pink, strapless gown with a flowing skirt that required a hoop to hold the skirt out around the bottom. Our school did not have a prom in those years, so it was purchased for me to wear to the junior-senior banquet.

Granny was primarily responsible for the chickens, including the gathering of their eggs. Several times, when we had gotten baby chicks from the local hatchery, we kept the baby chicks upstairs in Granny's room until they were big enough to put out in the chicken lot. We moved the furniture out of the dormer in her room and made a place for the babies. Until the baby chicks got bigger, it was such fun to go into Granny's room and play with those little baby chicks.

Granny Duvall contributed greatly by watching us children while Mama was working outside in the fields or in the garden. While Mama, Daddy, and all us kids might start out working on the farm, Granny would often start supper. And when I was old enough, and since I was the oldest girl, I was often sent in from the fields to help her with cooking and with setting the table. We often rang the big, old dinner bell on the pole near the house to let those who were still working know that supper was ready. If any family member heard that dinner bell, whether they were working outside in the fields or at other times playing back at the creek, in the barn, or in the yard, we knew we had better head to the house. We all were expected to be at the house at dinnertime. The dinner bell was our version of a cell phone!

Growing up, we always ate at the table together. When any meal was ready, our entire family ate at the same time. There was no taking a plate to eat in your room or in front of the TV, or sleeping in through breakfast. Eating together was a family affair, and no special allowances were made for any of us who might not like what we were having to eat. We ate whatever we liked that was on the table, or we did without. It was thought—and we were sometimes told—that if we got hungry enough, we would eat what had been cooked or what was on the table. There were no special allowances made, and there was *no complaining*!

With our large family, when we had fried chicken for supper, one chicken had to make many pieces. Before frying the chicken, Mama cut the chicken so everyone could have a piece to eat. There was the breast, the pulley bone, two wings, two thighs, two legs, the neck, the back, the gizzard, and the liver to be shared. Mama always saw that Daddy got the breast, which was his favorite piece and thought by many to be the best piece. Granny Duvall liked the liver, and she ate that. Brenda and I both liked the gizzard, and to forego an argument, we had to take turns getting to eat it.

Brenda and I both still like chicken gizzards today. Sometimes, I even buy a whole package and cook them. Mama always said her favorite piece was the neck, but thinking back, I think she was just unselfishly seeing that all of her family was taken care of before herself. That's the kind of mother she was! Always unselfish and thinking of others first!

I feel sure—if God keeps a ledger—Mama's name is on it!

9

In her last few years, and after I married and moved out, I didn't see Granny Duvall as much as I previously had seen her, but she had always been very important to me while I was still living at home. In her latter days, after she fell down the stairs and broke her leg, she was basically never the same, and she eventually ended up in a nursing home.

I went to the nursing home to see Granny quite often, and I took my young boys with me. She would always perk up when the boys came around. All the nursing home residents enjoyed seeing the young children. Seeing them in all their cuteness always brought smiles to their faces.

Granny's final demise came when she had to have both of her legs amputated due to the onset of gangrene. It broke my heart one day when I went to the hospital to see her, and she pulled up the covers to show me she no longer had legs. She didn't last much longer after that traumatic experience, and she died at the age of ninety-three.

Granny Duvall was always special to me in a personal way. Her room was upstairs, next to mine, and it was often a place of solace to me. Being the oldest girl, I was treated more strictly by Daddy when it came to what he let his children do and who we did them with. Even when his thinking might have been less than reasonable, I knew better than to question his decisions. So the choice I made was to do what Daddy said.

When I was being disciplined or felt unhappy about something, Granny had a way of making me feel better. I might go into her room feeling upset, looking for sympathy, or hoping she would take up for me or see my side, but she would just be kind and gentle without saying a word against Daddy. I never, *ever* remember her taking my side of an argument or siding with me as to how unfair Daddy or Mama might have been to me. Instead, she might just tell me to sit down for a minute, and she would talk about something else. I would sit down on a stool in front of her big chair by the window, and she would brush or braid my hair or rub some of her Pond's beauty cream on my hands or face until I calmed down. She would just *listen* when I was upset, showing a gentle and kind spirit, sometimes without even saying a word.

I think my memories of some of these special private times I had spent with Granny Duvall are why, when I first found out I was going to be a grandmother myself, I secretly hoped that my own grandchildren would someday think of me and remember me as fondly and lovingly as I remembered her.

When Alan and Lou Ann were having their first child, which would be my first grandchild, Lou Ann asked me one day what I wanted to be called after the baby was born. They said it was my choice. After thinking for a few minutes, I said I wanted to be called Granny. And just to be somewhat distinguishable, I specifically chose Granny Pat. And I've been called Granny Pat for over thirty years now, as Addison (my oldest grandchild), in his own cute, little way, started calling me that.

Since then, my six other grandchildren have been born—Bradley, Landon, Alana, Brooklyn, Allison, and Elijah, to whom I am also known as Granny Pat. They all were born within a ten-year period to three different sons. Today, I am also known as Granny Pat to my three great-grandchildren—Kobi, Kersi, and Bronx, with hopefully more to come.

I have loved being a grandmother, and being called Granny Pat has always been music to my ears! Those words encompass some of my most precious memories. It was special to me to have Granny Duvall living with us when I was growing up, and I only hope my own grandchildren will think as lovingly and kindly toward me as I feel when I think of her.

THREE

Work on the Farm

Hard work was always a part of life on the farm, from the time we moved there. From the time we were big enough, and even in elementary school, we had chores to do.

The following Bible verse must have been one of my parents' core beliefs:

> ...The one who is unwilling to work shall not eat.
> —Thessalonians 3:10 NIV

It sure seemed to apply to our family!

There was seemingly always work to do on the farm, both before and after school. I had friends who didn't want to come home and spend the night with me because they knew they would probably have to help me work. Sometimes, when they would come, they would want to go home after a while, and Daddy would end up taking them home.

At times, I thought I was being mistreated for having to work so hard when my friends did not, and even though I might have thought it, I did not say it. I do not remember any of us kids ever questioning or complaining about anything we were asked to do, especially by Daddy.

Daddy most likely would not be in compliance with some of the child labor laws of today. He might be accused of not abiding by these laws for insisting that we work so many hours every day while we were young students, but we kids understood who was in charge, and we just did what we were told to do. Family participation was expected and demanded.

Daddy had borrowed money to buy the farm from a businessman who was a Hardin County banker. After he had been turned down for a loan by others, Daddy had finally found someone to take a chance on him. This particular banker had faith in Daddy, and he became a frequent visitor to our farm. For years (maybe initially to check on his investment), he visited quite often. He and his wife grew to respect Mama and Daddy, how they were making improvements to the farm, how hard we were all working to make ends meet, and how Daddy was handling his business affairs. He also admired all of Mama's household and homemaking talents.

Even though Mama and Daddy didn't have many luxuries, and the banker and his wife were fairly well-off financially, they all became good friends, and in later years, they enjoyed visiting with each other, eating out together, and going to the banker's condo on the beach for visits together. The families might have been considered to be in very different social circles, but because of their kindnesses to each other and their mutual respect for each other, they became *lifelong* friends.

During my elementary years, while attending George H. Goodman Elementary School for six years, there was work to do both before and after school on the farm.

Many days after school were spent picking up rocks on the five hundred-acre farm and loading them in a trailer, trying to get them off the land to make it more tillable, so as not to damage the farm machinery.

Tobacco was one of the main money crops on the farm, and there were many different seasonal jobs to do that were connected with growing it. Many days were spent carrying brush for burning a tobacco bed. After the bed was burned, all the embers were cleared off, the seeds were planted, the beds were watered, and the canvas was put on the bed. Then we waited for the tobacco plants to grow.

After the plants grew to the right size, we pulled the tobacco plants out of the tobacco bed and set them out in rows in our fields. If it was too wet when the plants were ready, we had to peg out the tobacco, rather than using the tractor-pulled setter. One of my chores was riding the tobacco setter. I remember getting sick several times from smelling the tractor fumes, until Daddy finally fixed a long exhaust pipe that went upward to keep the fumes from going into my face. I could feed the setter with my left hand, which was harder for some of the others to do, so I was often needed to help on the tobacco setter.

As it was growing, we had to hoe the tobacco to keep the weeds out, we had to sucker it, we had to top it, and we had to worm it. Sometimes, work could be fun, such as worming the tobacco, when I would pull a big, juicy green tobacco worm off the plant and throw it on my sister Brenda. It was fun to hear her squeal!

We also had to cut the tobacco, spear it, load it on the trailer, and house it in the barn rafters.

So as not to waste any of the tobacco, we had to pick up what we called the "ground leaves" that had grown on the bottom of the stalks and sometimes might have fallen off. When needed, picking up ground leaves was one of the chores I had to do before I went to school. This had to be done while the dew was still on. It was necessary to go through the tobacco patch early in the morning and pick up those leaves so they wouldn't dry out and crumble. After doing that very early in the morning, I would go inside, wash up, and get ready to go on to school for the day.

It was stripping time after the tobacco crop had cured and come "in case." When the time was right, and the tobacco was in case, we took it off the rafters in the barn, bulked it, and were ready to start stripping.

All the stripping was done by hand, and often in the barn, where it was very cold. Sometimes, we had to wear gloves because it was so cold. We made five different grades—trash, lugs, bright leaf, dark leaf, and tips. It took most of the family members at stripping time, as one person pulled leaves off the tobacco stalk, which was their assigned grade, and passed it on to the next person in line at the stripping table.

When we had enough for a "hand," we tied the hand with another tobacco leaf, and put it on a tobacco stick to be hung back in the barn rafters. Then we waited until it was in case again to bulk it down and take it to the market to sell.

After the tobacco was sold, the proceeds were used in part for our Christmas money. We always had good things to eat for Christmas—lots of fruits, nuts, and candy that had been purchased at the local stockyards. There were big baskets of apples, oranges, or tangerines under the Christmas tree, different kinds of nuts in a bowl with a nutcracker for us to crack the nuts ourselves, and we *always* had chocolate drops.

I don't remember having many toys under the tree in those early years. I never got a doll for Christmas, but one year there *was* a special joint gift for us all: a new bicycle (a boy's bicycle). This was the same bicycle that, years later, we unsuccessfully tried to teach Mama to ride. We finally got her to try one Sunday afternoon, but she rolled down the hill and into the electric fence and lay there getting shocked. Needless to say, she didn't try again.

In farm families, neighbors helped neighbors! Most of our neighbors had tobacco crops. When we didn't have enough plants of our own, we shared with each other. Helping with the work was also shared. I was often "loaned out" to help. I helped neighbors either by pulling plants, setting out the tobacco plants, or later on, helping them to strip the tobacco. During those years, neighbors supported each other in many other ways besides helping with the tobacco crop. We shared our garden vegetables. We shared fresh meats whenever we killed hogs or processed our beef. We supported each other in times of sorrow. I remember the time when one of our neighbors had died, and we all went over to his house for the wake. Bodies were sometimes kept at home during those years, and visitation was done in the home of the deceased. It was somewhat unsettling for me, as a young girl, as I remember being so scared, and I did not want to even be in the same room with the dead body.

Another crop we grew on the farm was corn. In some years, gathering the corn could prove to be a major job. If the weather didn't cooperate, and the tractor couldn't go through, we sometimes went row by row with hoes to keep the weeds out. I remember once when it was so hot and we had worked in the sun all day, hoeing out the corn. I felt so sick that I could hardly stand. I was accused of just trying to get out of work, but I really wasn't. (At least, not that time.) Daddy let me go sit under a tree for a few minutes to rest, but I didn't get out of any work, as when I began to feel better, I still had to finish hoeing my rows of corn.

Not having modern machinery, such as there is today, when the corn was ready, we went through the rows of corn, picked it, and threw it in piles on the ground a few feet apart. Then we went through the corn patch and put the piles of corn in a trailer, hauled it out of the patch, and got it ready for market.

We grew wheat on the farm, but that was a crop we kids had little to do with. Daddy hired someone to harvest the wheat, but one year when the wheat had been combined and was put into bags, we kids actually *were* all needed to help. Daddy said the wheat was "going through a heat," and he was worried that it could ruin and wouldn't be good for selling if that happened.

We cleaned all the furniture out of the downstairs room where my two younger sisters slept. We took the bags of hot wheat, one by one, into their bedroom and poured out all the wheat in the bags all over the bedroom floor. Daddy had us kids walk through the wheat barefooted, over and over and over, to try to cool the wheat. When it had cooled enough, we put the wheat back into the bags and it was taken to market. The wheat crop was saved! In that instance, necessity really had proven to be the mother of invention!

For me, one of the hardest jobs that we did on the farm was what we called "picking pickles." Cucumbers were one of our cash crops. Most of the work was done in the hot summer months while we were out of school for the summer. There was a lot of bending over for long periods of time, and the cucumbers scratched and stained our hands, and it was usually so very hot out there in the pickle patch.

After the cucumbers were picked, they had to be bagged and taken to the pickle station in Clarkson, Kentucky, where they were put on a conveyor belt which graded them from smallest to largest. The very largest cucumbers, which were worth nothing, were taken back home and given to the hogs. The smallest cucumbers were the most valuable. They brought the most money per pound, but of course, it took more small cucumbers to make a pound.

After the pickles sold, we kids were given some of the money from the sale, which we were expected to use mostly to buy any needed school supplies, or a new pair of shoes for school or church.

Milking the cows was another one of our farm chores. If it wasn't my day to milk the cows, I had to go out to the pasture and drive the cows to the barn so my brother or sister could milk them. Our daily beverage of choice was milk. Daddy loved buttermilk, so we also had buttermilk. The milk was skimmed for cream, we churned our own butter, and Mama even made cottage cheese.

Another chore that needed to be done was slopping the hogs. We saved all the table scraps, potato peelings, soured milk, and anything else we couldn't eat to take to the hogs and pour in their trough. Shearing the sheep was always done by my older brother, and gathering the eggs was usually done by Granny. Everyone in the family worked!

Most of our food was either grown or raised on the farm. Until my high school days, the only restaurants I ever remember going to were Blue Boar and White Castle, and then only occasionally, when we had to go to Louisville for some reason.

We always had a large garden with all kinds of vegetables, and during the summer, we did lots of canning and freezing. There was practically no vegetable we didn't grow. We grew lettuce, onions, radishes, tomatoes, white potatoes, sweet potatoes, carrots, peas, bush beans, pole beans, corn, okra, cucumbers, asparagus, broccoli, and more. Everyone in the family worked in the garden from the time it was planted until it was all harvested. We hoed, picked, and gathered the vegetables and helped to prepare them for eating, canning, or freezing.

We grew strawberries, blackberries, gooseberries, rhubarb, watermelon, cantaloupe, and peanuts, and we had our own grape vines.

We had fruit orchards with apple, pear, and peach trees. The peach trees served a dual purpose, as often this was where the switches came from which were used on us when we misbehaved. Sometimes, we had to go out and break off the peach tree limb that was going to be used for our own whipping, so it helped when we could find a limb with no nodules. The limb was then smoother, and it would hurt less when we were struck. Family discipline measures were not questioned as I was growing up, even though that form of discipline might be considered by some as child abuse, if it were used today.

We killed hogs for meat, from which came the delicious, fresh tenderloin and country ham. We also made souse. (Don't ask!) Let's just say, Spam is better! We ate fish caught in our pond, the favorites being bass and bluegill. We had cows for beef, which made hamburgers, roasts, and steaks.

Before we had a home freezer, we kept as much meat as possible in the freezer compartment of the refrigerator. We kept the rest of the processed meat in a locker plant in Elizabethtown. When we needed more meat at home, we made trips to Elizabethtown to the locker plant, where the meat was stored until we needed it. When our home freezer was empty, we would make a trip to the locker plant and bring a little more meat home until we could afford to buy our own freezer.

We raised our own chickens and killed our own chickens to eat. There was a big stump by the basement door where Mama would cut off the chicken's head. None of us kids liked to do that, so Mama would do it. Mama would then scald the chickens, and we kids would help to pick off the feathers and get them cleaned and ready for frying.

Everyone in our family worked hard when necessary. Mama was one of the hardest workers you could ever find, working both inside and outside the house on the farm. Daddy worked hard. He had a route as a rural mail carrier, would come home and rest for a while, and would then start back to work doing some job on the farm. He sometimes would be at school as soon as the bell rang, he'd pick us up, and we would all go home and work together. We wasted no daylight hours!

Mama and Daddy worked *with us* when we were learning to do farm tasks and different kinds of work on the farm. They didn't just tell us what to do and leave us to do it on our own. We learned hard work by their examples!

As younger children, we might not have liked it at the time, and many times, I thought we should not have been expected to work so hard, as other kids did not have to do all the chores we had to do on the farm. However, as an adult, I appreciate that lifelong quality that was instilled within us all as we worked together and grew up together on the farm. We all learned the *value and rewards of hard work*, which carried over into the adult lives of my siblings and myself. Sadly, I fear that same work ethic is missing in the lives of many young people today.

F O U R

Fun on the Farm

Not all was work on the farm!

We did many interesting and fun things, and we had adventures that some kids and their parents might even *pay* to do now. Even though we did not have a lot of money or purchased items to play with, we learned how to entertain ourselves. We learned how to improvise. We learned about nature and how to enjoy nature. We learned survival skills. We learned how valuable just resting is, after a day of hard work.

Under today's rules, our family would probably qualify for welfare and get lots of government assistance, but I really didn't think of us then as being poor. We were actually rich in many important aspects of life! I even liked the tomato sandwiches with Miracle Whip for lunch, and the goldenrod eggs we often had for supper.

There were, admittedly, times when I wished I had some of the things I saw other people have, or could do what others could do, such as getting a perm at the beauty shop instead of my mother giving me a home perm, or buying a pretty dress instead of Granny making them from feed sacks, or always having snacks and candy around to eat (which we didn't have).

I used to think my best friend was rich, because every time I spent the night with her, her mother would buy a whole bag of Reese's peanut butter cups and would let us eat all we wanted. Nothing like that ever happened at my house. That was such a treat when I was at her house.

She and I were both Big Clifty girls. Her mother worked with my daddy. Daddy was a rural mail carrier, and her mother was the postmaster.

We went to school together, spent nights together, played together, talked about our boyfriends, and learned together.

One thing we learned on our own was the "deaf and dumb" alphabet. We used it to talk to a lady near where my best friend lived. We would walk out a country road to the lady's house and would talk to her. We knew the signs for the letters, and we spelled out the words for her on our hands. Knowing how to spell with this alphabet not only helped us connect with this lady, but it also came in handy, even in high school, when we were sometimes in class and the teacher had declared, "No talking!" As friends, we could continue to communicate. Even today, I still remember and can make on my hands all the signs for the letters of that alphabet.

When we had free time on the farm, we would often fix ourselves peanut butter sandwiches and head back to the Petty Blue Hole, which was a creek on the back of our property. We would stay away from the house for hours and hours. We would cut our own cane fishing poles, we would fish in the creek, dig our own worms, play in the water and caves, look for Indian arrowheads, eat wild grapes along the way, swing on the grape vines, chew on sassafras, and just have fun in the outdoors.

No one seemed to worry about us or be overprotective if we were gone for hours and hours, just as long as we always managed to get back to the house by suppertime and before dark.

We had the pond in which to fish and swim. Daddy even built us a diving board at the pond. It was fun to swim and cool off in the pond on a hot summer day. At least it was fun to swim and cool off in the pond, until I pulled in a huge turtle one day. I almost had the turtle to the shore on my fishing pole when it snapped the line and swam back into the water. Swimming in the pond wasn't quite so much fun for me after that, even though it *was* still fun to continue to fish.

On any given day, when we were not working, we might play in and around the barn, climbing on the rafters or daring each other to jump out of the barn loft. We might go out to the barn to grind corn for the chickens, bottle-feed the baby lambs, give something to the cows in the stalls to eat, or call the hogs to see if we could get them to come to the trough. We learned to love and appreciate all the farm animals, and we had names for many of them. Minerva Bess (nicknamed Minnie Bess) was one of our best milk cows.

Sometimes, we might be found cracking walnuts on a rock, picking out the kernels with a nail, and saving the kernels for Mama to put into her divinity candy or one of her other delicious desserts. There was always something to do, or we would find or invent something to do. We had a basketball goal in the gravel area near the barn, where we would often be if we had free time. At times, we would ride our bicycle (without a helmet), or play yard games such as badminton, horseshoes, croquet, or softball.

We had a playhouse in the back of the chicken yard. That was a perfect place to play under all the big shade trees. We made furniture from rocks and scraps of wood and used big, empty grapefruit juice cans for seating. Our imagination and creativity were constantly bringing us new fun and adventures.

We had no computers, cell phones, or video games, and for several years, no TV. Before we got a TV for ourselves, we would usually go over to an aunt and uncle's house on Friday night and watch wrestling. My favorite wrestler was known as Pretty Boy. It was also entertaining to watch the commercials between rounds when Myrtle, the Oertel turtle, would strut across the screen, saying "I'm Myrtle, the Oertel turtle!" She was advertising Oertel's '92 beer, which was brewed in the Louisville, Kentucky plant.

I don't think Mama and Daddy ever knew it, but I sometimes tried things which I knew they probably wouldn't like. I once tried to roll my own cigarette with some of the tobacco leaves that were hanging in the barn. And another time, I made a corncob pipe, crushed up some tobacco leaves, and tried to smoke it. Basically, tobacco made me sick, so those experiments didn't last long. My experimentation with drugs was confined to that!

I think Mama and Daddy recognized and appreciated that we kids helped out a lot. We had to! But they helped to make us feel rewarded and appreciated in little ways. After working hard and having our baths, and even when we had on our pajamas, Daddy sometimes might take us downtown to the local drugstore, let us sit on stools, and would buy us an ice cream cone and would brag on how hard we had worked that day. Little things like that seemed to help. It took a little of the unpleasantness out of working so hard, when we felt like we were being rewarded for our work.

The year my older brother was to graduate from high school, and when

I was a junior in high school, we took our *one and only* family vacation. As I remember, Daddy said he wanted us all to have a trip together while we kids were all still at home together. We had never taken a family vacation, and Daddy said we were going to have one, even if he had to borrow the money for us to go.

We loaded the station wagon, with the luggage and supplies on top, with six kids and Mama and Daddy riding inside, and headed west. The back seat of the station wagon faced the rear, and as we rode along, three of us were usually riding in the back seat with our feet hanging out the back window. We were going to visit an aunt who lived in Oakland, California, at the time. On the way to California, we took a northern route to sightsee and visit relatives along the way. We stopped in Colorado Springs, drove up to Pikes Peak, and headed on to Denver, stopping at the Air Force Academy and visiting with Uncle Lewis.

We drove through the beautiful Rocky Mountain National Park, enjoying the beautiful Colorado scenery. We might stop by a little mountain stream just long enough for Mama to fry bacon and eggs, or for us to eat peanut butter and jelly sandwiches. For our family of eight, we spent very little on food.

We drove on in Wyoming through Grand Teton National Park and Yellowstone National Park, where we saw fascinating sights. We saw many animals, such as bears and bison, Yellowstone Falls, Yellowstone Lake, and hot springs of boiling water, including the Old Faithful geyser, which we saw shoot off right on schedule.

On we went through Montana and Idaho, stopping in Rexburg, Idaho, where we saw the JC Penney store that an uncle had owned years before. In Idaho, we passed the Atomic Energy Commission's testing grounds, and saw lava fields at Craters of the Moon.

We drove along the Oregon Trail toward Portland, along the beautiful Columbia River Basin. We stopped at Portland and visited with relatives, then traveled on to Cutler City, Oregon, to visit another aunt and uncle. Our uncle in Cutler City was the only one home at the time, as our aunt had gone to Canada and Alaska.

As we entered California, we drove along the Redwood Highway and stopped to see many giant redwood trees, one of which was big enough to drive a car through, and of course, we had to do that.

Nine days after leaving home, we arrived at my aunt's house in Oakland, California. We stayed there for eight days, and while there, we were treated to some of the nearby attractions. We went to the beach at Santa Cruz, swam in the Pacific Ocean, and went to Golden Gate Park, the Golden Gate Bridge, the San Francisco Zoo and Aquarium of the Bay, the Japanese Tea Garden, Fairyland, and the San Francisco International Airport.

Time had passed so quickly. We had a wonderful time, and before starting back home, we went to Los Angeles. We saw some of the movie stars' homes in Beverly Hills and Hollywood, as well as some of the famous Hollywood places, such as Ciro's, the Paramount Theatre, the Globe and Hollywood theaters, the Hollywood Roosevelt and Knickerbocker hotels, 20th Century Studios, and Capitol recording studios, among many other sites. We then headed on to Knott's Berry Farm on the way to Disneyland, and enjoyed several hours there.

We took a southern route as we headed back home, driving across the Arizona desert at nighttime. After leaving Flagstaff and passing Arizona State University, we headed for the Grand Canyon, which was one of the highlights of the trip. The scenery there was awesome! The colors, the shapes of the rocks, and the lay of the ground, the canyon, and the canyon gorges were absolutely breathtaking! It is such a unique part of our wonderful country!

We drove across the Painted Desert through Petrified Forest National Park, and took pictures with some little Navajo boys who demanded money from us. After giving them some change, we drove on. Our last stop in Arizona was to climb to the top of Sunset Crater, which was an old volcano that had erupted many years before.

We drove all the next day through the rest of Arizona, across New Mexico, through Albuquerque, and across the Texas Panhandle, and then started across Oklahoma on the Oklahoma Turnpike.

After leaving Oklahoma, we drove across Missouri and across the tip of Illinois to the town of Cairo, where the Ohio River runs into the Mississippi River. A few miles later, we were back in Kentucky. We spent the night in Paducah, about fifteen miles from Kentucky Dam, and enjoyed accommodations more spacious and luxurious than any other place we had stayed since we had started on our trip. With Daddy and my older brother alternating as drivers, we had not stopped driving since leaving Winslow, Arizona.

We enjoyed a leisurely next day swimming at Kentucky Lake before starting back to Big Clifty, where we were very happy to once again see Granny and our dog, Flash. Except for three flat tires, we had thoroughly enjoyed a wonderful, once-in-a-lifetime, three-week family vacation, and we created many lifelong memories together. Our parents' wish had been fulfilled! Before any of my brothers and sisters had graduated from high school and started on our own individual paths, we had enjoyed a family vacation together.

By this time, the farm where we lived was basically cleared and producing crops. We had animals grazing in the pastures in the fields all over the farm. We gradually had more leisure time and could afford to buy a few more pieces of farm equipment or other items of choice. We no longer had to spend as much time doing the hard work that we had done on the farm for so many of the earlier years. There was a better balance of work and play, and farm life became much more enjoyable and satisfying—and the choices made for us by our parents were not nearly as demanding as in earlier years.

The farm in Big Clifty, Kentucky, was a good place to grow up!

FIVE

Early School Years

As hard as we might have worked on the farm, education was always a priority.

Even though we didn't stay home to do farm work, and we got up early to do our chores before going to school, we didn't miss school to work, and we got to school on time. Daddy would take us to school, and if there was work to do, he would be there to pick us up as soon as the bell rang to let us out in the afternoon.

No daylight hours were wasted by riding home on the bus if there was work to do. To ease the pain of having to work after school, before we went out to the fields to work after we got home, there was usually an afternoon snack waiting for us. As soon as we walked in the door, we could often smell the gingerbread that Mama or Granny had just taken out of the oven.

After supper, if I had homework, instead of doing one of my nightly chores (which was helping with the dishes), Mama would often do my part if I told her I had homework to do.

Occasionally, I might clean up, wash, and dry the dishes all by myself as my sister Brenda hated doing the dishes so badly, she would sometimes give me her whole week's allowance of a quarter just to get out of her chore one time.

I would often save that quarter until I could go to town in Big Clifty to a little local grocery store (Elsie Mae's) and buy a box of raisins or a giant Baby Ruth candy bar. I could make either of them last all week, while upstairs in my room reading my modern romance comic books or listening to *The Lone Ranger* on the radio, with Zelzepay, my three-legged cat, laying on the bed beside me, and with my prized poster of Robert Wagner on the wall.

One of Mama's main contributions to our education was that she was a good speller, and remained so throughout her life. She had been a county champion speller in her own right when she was young. She always encouraged us to be in our school spelling bees, and she spent many hours giving out words for us to spell at home for practice.

As a result, my siblings and I won spelling bees both at our grade levels as well as countywide. When I was in the seventh grade, I won the county spelling championship by spelling the word *acknowledgment*. As the county champion, I received a trophy, a ribbon, and a twenty-five-dollar savings bond, which I later used to buy my husband's wedding band. My own three boys followed in their grandmother's and my footsteps, as they were also good spellers and entered and won spelling bees themselves.

In our academic endeavors, not only were we expected to be good spellers, but we were also expected to be all-around good students. Daddy was the one who signed our report cards. Each six-week grading period, he would look at them carefully and review them with us before signing them. During these school years, we were not only graded in subject areas, but also in conduct, effort, and citizenship as well. Daddy wanted to see all As and complimented and bragged on us if we got them. Anything else had to be explained, and I never, ever wanted to disappoint Daddy.

For the most part, these high expectations from Mama and Daddy must have contributed to our learning and produced good results, as my five siblings and I all ended up being either valedictorian or salutatorian of our high school graduating classes.

My first six years of school were spent at George H. Goodman Elementary School in Big Clifty, Kentucky, which in those years consisted of first through sixth grades. At that country school, we received a good foundation for future learning and achievement, and school was actually fun—much more fun than working on the farm. I really loved school!

I have very few memories of first and second grade, which were in a combined classroom. I know I got a good start in reading, but one of the memories that does come to mind was when a classmate jumped out of the window of our upper-story classroom one day and got into trouble with the teacher.

Later, in third and fourth grade, we were encouraged to enter class contests and spelling bees. If we were the classroom spelling winner, the teacher would let us go out and sit on the steps and give out words to each other, as long as we were finished with our classwork assignments. One memorable fall, our class was tasked with a project, which was identification of leaves, and we had beautiful fall-colored leaves hanging on lines all across our classroom.

In 1952, in my third- and fourth-grade classroom, we did a political canvass of the presidential election with Adlai Stevenson, the Democrat, and Dwight D. Eisenhower, the Republican, running for president. In our classroom, Eisenhower won; and later, in November, he won the actual presidential election in a landslide victory. That might have been my first noted introduction to politics.

As we progressed through those days at George H. Goodman, we built a good foundation for learning, but we had fun at school as well. There was always a recess time when we could go out in the schoolyard and play. All six grades at the school had recess at the same time. The bigger kids watched after the little kids, several of whom might have been little brothers or sisters.

At George H. Goodman, we played different games from day to day and from group to group. Some of them included: tag, hopscotch, leapfrog, jump rope, ring around the rosy, duck duck goose, hide and seek, marbles, dodge ball, flying Dutchman, kick the can, red rover, and blind man's bluff.

There were no indoor bathrooms at George H Goodman. On the left-hand side of the building, and some distance behind the school building, was the girls' toilet, and on the right-hand side of the building, some distance behind the building, was the boys' toilet. Almost every Halloween, one of the local pranks was to turn over those outdoor toilets.

For several years, our family brought our lunches to school in brown paper bags or lunchboxes. Many days, our lunch might be a sausage and biscuit and maybe an apple. A time or two, I remember trading my sausage and biscuit with a friend for a bologna sandwich and thinking what a good trade I had made. Each of us had a collapsible tin cup with a lid that opened and closed down like an accordion, which we filled with water from the one drinking fountain in the upstairs hallway at the school. Water was always our lunchtime beverage!

At first, Daddy and Mama couldn't really afford to pay for all of us kids to eat in the school lunchroom, but we later *did* stop bringing our lunches and got to eat in the lunchroom, which was in the school basement. However, we did not get free lunches or even reduced-price lunches, as many children do today. Since we were both good students, my older brother and I were allowed to work, so the school-age kids in our family could all eat in the lunchroom. My brother's job was to fire the big, old coal furnace in the dirty coal room in the basement, and my job was to set the lunchroom table and clean off all the tables after lunch. At George H. Goodman, we worked in exchange for our school lunches.

There was no complaint about separation of church and state in our school at that time. All fifth- and sixth-grade students were required weekly to memorize a Bible verse, then stand up before the class and say the Bible verse every Friday after we said the Pledge of Allegiance. It didn't matter if you said the same one you had said the week before, or (as some did) if you said the shortest verse in the Bible many times. One popular example was from John 11:35, KJV "Jesus wept."

Every student was always expected to participate, and *everyone did*!

Our teacher would also say a Bible verse. The one I remember her saying more than once was in Matthew 23:37, KJV: "O Jerusalem, Jerusalem, thou that killest the prophets, and stonest them which are sent unto thee, how often would I have gathered my children together, even as a hen gathereth her chickens under her wings, and ye would not!" I had no idea what that really meant at the time, but the verse stuck with me.

Later in life, I looked it up and surmised that the meaning was that Jesus wants to save us, just as he wanted to save the Jews, but in spite of all the drawing desires and actions of God, God's grace can never overcome the stubborn will of man, unless man chooses to cooperate.

We had extracurricular activities while at George H. Goodman before the idea of them being separate subjects was even popular. Along with music (singing mostly folk and patriotic songs at all grade levels), we had PE (recess outside, playing many different games), art and theater (selected drawings and school plays), and literature (we had to memorize lots of poems). We also were required to memorize significant parts of historical documents, such as the preamble to the Constitution and the Gettysburg Address. Integration of all these activities made school and learning a lot of fun for us as elementary students at this little country school, and I still remember many of the things we were taught there.

I do not remember many discipline problems while at George H. Goodman, but there *was* always the risk of getting hit across the wrist or hand with a ruler if we misbehaved. There was also the awareness of a paddle on the teacher's desk or somewhere in the classroom. We had no PTA, and no parent-teacher conference days, or site-based council meetings, but most of us knew that if we ever got into trouble at school, we would also have to answer to our parents when we got home. That usually proved to be a good motivator for following the rules and good behavior. Knowing that usually helped us to make good choices.

SIX

Middle School and High School

I started at Clarkson School in Clarkson, Kentucky, when I was in the seventh grade, and Clarkson School was quite a new experience. At that time, grades one through twelve were at that same location. I was developing new and varied interests, including crushes on boys. My first date was going to the county fair and riding the rides with a boy. That was like pre-dating, when a boy you liked would ask you to meet him at the Grayson County Fair and ride the rides with him. Not many months ago, I remembered my first pre-date when I heard that the wife of the boy I had gone to the fair with sixty-eight years ago had passed away.

Seventh and eighth grades at Clarkson began a time of further development in my learning process. The main thing I remember about seventh grade was my homeroom teacher, who could really make a piano sing. My eighth-grade teacher was a very strict teacher, but a good teacher. If you were a student in her class, you learned!

There was one grading period during my eighth-grade year when I thought I was really going to be in trouble with Daddy. The teacher said she was going to give me an F in conduct. I had been in line with a group of students who were waiting at her desk while she was out of the room. The person who was in front of the line proceeded to open the teacher's record book and was looking in it, giving us all our recorded grades. About that time, our teacher walked back into the room. She considered everyone in line guilty, and she was going to give us all Fs in conduct for that six-week period for looking in her record book while she was out of the classroom.

She *did* tell us there was a way we could get that F off our report card, if we wanted to get it changed. To do that, she said we would need to memorize the Sermon on the Mount (Matthew 5–7 in the New Testament). There were—and still are—many good lessons taught by Jesus in those passages, but memorizing all three chapters seemed like a little much for just looking in a teacher's record book. I had a hard choice to make. Either I memorized those three chapters, or I had to tell Daddy why I was getting an F in conduct.

I decided to tell him. Thankfully, he agreed that the punishment was a little much, and I was so happy and relieved that he didn't make me memorize those chapters. So, with his understanding, that six-week period, I got all As, except in conduct and effort. I never did quite understand how I could get As in all my subjects and still get a B in effort, but I was told that getting good grades just seemed to come too easily to me and that I could get an A without trying. Since it was believed that I did not have to put forth much effort, I would not be given an A in effort. I didn't really agree with that, as no one else had any idea how many hours I actually spent studying at home.

Some of my most memorable seventh- and eighth-grade activities were the school fairs. At that time, there were three county schools: Clarkson, Leitchfield, and Caneyville. We had an annual school fair with academic and athletic competitions. There was also someone who would be crowned as the school fair queen each year. This was not in any way a beauty contest, but the winner was simply the girl who had raised the most money for our school.

During the school fairs, both in our classrooms and in the hallways, we would display our schoolwork. There were contests for the entries, such as penmanship. Those entries of penmanship writing samples were pinned on a clothesline in the hallways or rooms to be judged by outsiders, and the winners were awarded ribbons for first, second, and third places, according to how well they had followed the method of writing that had been taught.

Sixty years ago, there was quite an emphasis placed on neat and legible cursive writing, and most teachers had taken a required penmanship course at the teachers' college at Western (which is known today as Western Kentucky University). Teacher graduates then proceeded to teach their students. In recent years, little emphasis has been placed on cursive writing and good penmanship, and some young people today have trouble even reading cursive writing, much less writing legibly.

For those who liked sports and were athletically inclined, there were fun contests at the fairs, such as sack races, three-legged races, the fifty-yard dash, egg-throwing contests, baseball or softball throws, and long jumps and high jumps, among others. I won several of those contests, but my sister Brenda was a better athlete than I was, and she probably won more contests than I did. I didn't usually compete against Brenda, but in most of my contests, my main competition was a girl from another county school, who was a fabulous high school athlete. She was often the winner in many of the contests in which I was an entrant.

After finishing seventh and eighth grade, and before going into high school, we had to take what was called the diploma. After finishing eighth grade, we went to the Grayson County Courthouse in Leitchfield, Kentucky, and took the test in one of the courtrooms. We answered questions about various subject areas that we had previously studied up to that point in our educational careers. This resulted in a grade-level score supposedly to see whether we were ready to go to high school.

This would be the equivalent of a standardized test given today purporting to show readiness for a particular grade level. This was the only standardized test given at our school, and then only after eight years of school had been completed. It's hard to imagine, compared to all the testing done today in schools throughout our state and across the country.

Entering high school brought more changes. I then found myself wanting to look and dress a little differently, instead of wearing my basic, rolled-up jeans and keeping my short, boyish haircut. I was noticing how the girls looked and dressed in ways that most of the boys seemed to like, and I was wanting to look more like them. With my large family, I was aware that we had limited funds. I didn't have the luxury of store-bought dresses or outfits, and I didn't have the option of going to the beauty shop for a perm or hairstyle, as some of my classmates and friends did.

As a freshman, I wanted to be a cheerleader. With the election of cheerleaders to be held the upcoming school day, I was especially worried the night before. There were no tryouts at that time to determine who might do the best job as a cheerleader. It didn't matter which girls were more athletically inclined, or who could do acrobatics. Being elected cheerleader was basically a popularity contest with the student body voting for who they liked and wanted to be a cheerleader, and it often seemed to be the prettiest girls. Some of the girls who were running for cheerleader were going to the beauty shop to get their hair fixed in order to try to look especially good for the next day when the voting was to take place. I knew I couldn't go, but I *so much* wanted to look good too!

Seeing my disappointment, and trying to make me feel better and hopefully to make me look better, Mama somehow got a kit to give me a home perm herself the night before. Sadly, the perm turned out to be disastrous! I went to school the next day with frizzy hair, thinking I looked absolutely awful. Then the voting took place.

There would be five cheerleaders elected, and a freshmen could only be elected as a junior varsity cheerleader. I came in sixth in the voting and was devastated at not making the top five. As a very ungrateful young girl, I somehow blamed Mama for my loss because my perm had looked so awful. Even though Mama had gone the extra mile to lovingly try to make me feel like I also would look pretty the next day, at the time, I was very unappreciative! I was totally being an ungrateful brat! After fully realizing what she had tried to do, I later apologized and thanked her for all she had done. She had tried her best to make me feel prettier, and I should have appreciated her efforts.

Not being elected as a freshman cheerleader was one of my first major disappointments! Other disappointments, and more significant ones, would come later, but I *learned* from that disappointment.

If we never had any storms, we couldn't appreciate the sunshine.
—Dale Evans

Very shortly thereafter, one of the five girls who had been elected as a freshman cheerleader had to leave the cheerleading squad, and since I had come in sixth, I took her place and remained as a junior varsity cheerleader, and then as a varsity cheerleader, all throughout the rest of my high school years.

Cheerleading was basically the only physical activity for girls when I was in high school. There was no basketball team or any other sports team for girls. I would have loved that, but separate girls' sports were not available during my high school years. High school chorus and band became available soon after I graduated, and some of my younger siblings were fortunate to be able to participate in those activities a few years later.

I did have the opportunity to participate in some clubs. The 4-H club was one that I really enjoyed, and I learned a lot through some of the 4-H competitions. I once gave a winning demonstration on how to iron a man's shirt. I later won a county speech contest and got to represent my school and county at the state contest, which was on the University of Kentucky campus in Lexington. That was in the 1950s.

My speech was entitled "Will Communism Rule the World?" which was a question many in the public arena were asking at that time. The speech contest was a great experience for me. Although I did not win the state speech contest, I had a lot of fun, and meeting boys was an additional perk. While there in Lexington one night, I met a boy from another small Kentucky town whom I thought was really cute. I was super excited and very anxious to see him again the next morning. To my disappointment, when I saw him the next morning in broad daylight, he did not look nearly as good as he had the night before around the campfire. In that instance, my excitement was short-lived!

There were also cooking and sewing projects that, as 4-H members, we had the opportunity to learn and try. We were always encouraged to enter our projects in the 4-H exhibits at the local county fair each year, with the expectation of receiving ribbons and money. Some of these entries proved to be very rewarding.

The other club I enjoyed was the Tri-Hi-Y Club, which was basically centered around patriotism and American values. I think this may have been the beginning of the thinking that helped to shape my lifelong feelings about how fortunate I am to live in the United States of America, the greatest country in the world! Through activities in that club, I developed such respect for our American flag, and all our military members and the sacrifices they had made and are still making for us today.

It saddens me to see students today who have little historical knowledge of our founding documents and Constitution, and who lack respect for the flag of their own country, what it represents, and the men who have fought under it. Many students today have not been taught, or at least have not learned, how blessed they have been and how blessed they *are* to live in the

United States of America. Even with the blessing of being born here, there seems to be little appreciation for the freedoms enjoyed in America. At the same time, so many people from other countries are risking their lives and fortunes just to have the *opportunity* to enjoy those same freedoms.

Throughout my high school years, I had interests in several boys; some reciprocated, and others were not interested. There was always the talk about Clarkson girls dating Leitchfield or Caneyville boys, and that was frowned upon by some at our school, as our three county schools were rivals in sports. However, I seemed to end up dating more Caneyville and Leitchfield boys than boys at Clarkson. The ones at my own school who I might have been interested in seemed to be already taken.

English, math, health, and home economics were my favorite high school subjects. I had good teachers, and I liked them all.

I was around my health teacher quite a bit, as I was a cheerleader, and he was the high school coach of the Clarkson Red Hawks. He was such a good influence on all "his girls and boys," as he called us. Even after we graduated from high school, he always kept up with all his former players and cheerleaders. He was dearly loved by many. It is truly a testament to any teacher when they are fondly remembered as an important part of a student's learning experience.

Home economics class was a class where I began to learn many practical, lifelong skills. My home economics teacher was good at teaching us so many practical things that have carried over into my lifelong love of many homemaking activities. We learned manners, etiquette, how to serve and set a table in preparation for the junior-senior banquet, and how to sew (my first project was an apron). We cooked and baked and shared with others in the school, and we collected recipes for later use.

Even today, I still have some of my recipe cards from my little green recipe box that my home economics teacher had us start for future use. The recipes are some of the dishes we prepared and cooked in home economics class. I have had a special lifelong fondness for recipes and cookbooks, and today, I can sit and look through cookbooks and recipes from my present-day collection for hours at a time.

At Clarkson High School, in 1960, we did not have a high school prom, much less a middle school prom, as became more common a few years later in many schools. The junior-senior banquet was our big school event. The home economics girls who were juniors served the seniors at the banquet. Then, the next year, when the junior girls became seniors, they were served by the incoming junior home economics class.

All through high school, the different classes worked at the school fair, among other activities, trying to raise and save money for the senior trip. We had the opportunity during my high school years to be in special performances or plays which were presented to our parents and the public to help us raise money. During my senior year, our class presented a play called *A Hillbilly Weddin'*, in which I played a character named Ceelie Belsnickle.

After graduation, all seniors were offered the opportunity to go on a bus trip to Washington, DC, for a senior trip. Those who went were fortunate to see several historical sites in our nation's capital, which was a once-in-a-lifetime experience for many. Going to Washington, DC, with fellow classmates was a fun and educational experience. Additionally, I think that trip added to my sense of patriotism and helped me to appreciate even more the wonderful country in which I lived. As high school students, we had worked for four years throughout our high school years to save for our senior trip. To go was an easy choice for me, as that was my reward for my hard work, and the exciting culmination of our high school years together at Clarkson High School.

SEVEN

1960—A Monumental Year

Near the end of my senior year in high school, and shortly before my high school graduation, several important and life-changing events began to alter the trajectory of my life.

Going to church had always been an important part of our family life. We most always attended on Sunday mornings, Sunday nights, and Wednesday nights.

On a Wednesday night in the spring of 1960, I met Sam, my future husband, at the Clarkson Church of Christ. He had come to Wednesday-night Bible study with his friend. After church was over, the friend asked me if I could go to the Dairy Queen with them and let them bring me home later. Of course, I had to ask permission. Wanting to go, and thinking Daddy would not let me go by myself with strangers, I knew I would have a better chance of going if my sister and I both went together. I had hoped that with both of us going, Daddy would say yes. It worked! Daddy said it was OK since we *both* were going with the two of them. So my sister and I had a big date! We were going to the Dairy Queen after church that night.

I assumed that I would be going with Sam's friend, and my sister would be going along with Sam, since the friend had been the one who had initially asked *me* to go. But the strange thing about that date was that, at Sam's insistence, all four of us sat in the front seat of Sam's 1958 red Impala convertible, and somehow, I ended up sitting next to Sam (who was the driver), with my sister next to me, and Sam's friend on the outside. All four of us were riding in the front seat of the car.

We went to the Dairy Queen, which was *the hot spot* to go in 1960. We were having fun, circling the Dairy Queen and waving to our friends, while riding in Sam's red convertible. We were cool! The four of us had a good time laughing and talking, but Sam kept trying to get my attention by flipping my ponytail when no one was looking, and then pretending he hadn't done it. I knew he was flirting, but I thought he was cute, and I was attracted to him.

A few days later, he called me and told me he wanted to go out with me but didn't want to hurt his friend's feelings, since he knew his friend wanted to go out with me too. I didn't want to hurt the friend's feelings either, and I didn't want my sister to think I was trying to go out with *her* date. After talking about it, Sam and I decided to go out the next weekend. Since all any of the four of us had ever done together was to go to the Dairy Queen after church one night, we didn't see a problem with going out on a date with each other.

We instantly hit it off, and that date led to many phone calls and other dates. We had *one phone* in the house that the entire family had to share, and it was kept on a desk in the downstairs hallway. It was a black dial telephone which had a long cord, which thankfully, could stretch several feet. To get any privacy, we had to stretch it to the bathroom or bedroom and close the door to talk. With such limited time among the nine people living in the same household, I can remember making lists of things I wanted to be sure to talk to Sam about or say to him when he called. I didn't want to forget anything important when it was my turn to use the phone.

Shortly after meeting Sam, I finished high school and in the fall was planning to go to college at Lipscomb University in Nashville, Tennessee, where I had received an academic scholarship. Sam had finished a year at Western Kentucky University and was working at a local bank.

My college scholarship needed to be supplemented by other funds, so I was told by Daddy that I needed to get a job during the summer to save some money to help pay for some of my college expenses. I didn't have a car, and I had not gotten one for graduation, as is the expectation for many children today.

After high school graduation, and after returning from my senior trip, Daddy took me to Leitchfield one morning, dropped me off, and told me to find a job, and that he would be back to pick me up that afternoon. I went to several of the offices around the square and told several people in different businesses that I was looking for summer employment, but with no success.

Finally, I went to the courthouse and asked at the county clerk's office. The county clerk at the time was a Republican. At that time, I had not as yet registered to vote. I was told if I would register as a Republican that I had the job! I had a choice to make! I wanted a job! I needed a job! So I registered as a Republican, and I was hired for a summer job working in the record room at the county clerk's office. Even though that request might be frowned upon today, believe me, at that time, I was extremely grateful! I had good news when Daddy picked me up that afternoon. *I had a job!*

I saw Sam every day that summer as we were both working in the same town of Leitchfield. We were both working on the square, and we had lunch together every day. Daddy brought me to work every day, and Sam would bring me home after we both got off from work. We would put the top down on the convertible, drive around together, and have a good time just being together. We were together most nights and every weekend, and we also attended church together on Sunday mornings, Sunday nights, and Wednesday nights.

We fell in love that summer!

Daddy always had questions about the boys I wanted to date, and sometimes for whatever reason, I would not get to go out with them. He initially had questions for Sam, but Sam very patiently and kindly stood up to Daddy, and they came to respect each other very much. Daddy actually liked Sam. He could talk business with him. Daddy admired his business savvy, and they had a lot of good conversations when we had Sunday dinners together.

Sam had many meals with us, we took my sisters along sometimes when we went on dates, and we all went to church together. Sam was someone Daddy could talk to about business and financial matters, and he became almost like a part of our family even before we got married. Everyone in my family loved him! Mama was so accommodating to Sam that I often jokingly accused her of liking him better than she liked me. Daddy no longer seemed to question my going out with Sam, as he had with some of the other boys I'd wanted to date, even though most of those other boys were actually very nice.

As the time neared for me to start to college, Sam and I didn't want to be away from each other. Sam actually went to Lipscomb University, got a basketball scholarship, and was going to finish college there himself. We were planning to go to college there together that fall. However, his plans changed when he told the officers at the bank that he was planning to leave his position there. He was offered such a good raise and a promotion that he no longer felt like he could afford to leave.

Even though Sam was going to continue his work at the bank, I was still planning to go to college in the fall. I already had a part-time job in the audiovisual department at Lipscomb to help with my college expenses. Sam and I talked about getting married, but at my young age of seventeen, we knew we had to have parental consent. We went to Louisville together one day before I left for college, and we got rings without telling anyone. We were in love, and for a while, we were secretly engaged!

When I finally told Mama and Daddy I wanted to get married instead of going to college, Daddy was very angry, to say the least. He said that, if Sam really wanted to marry me, he would have already given me a ring. That was when I told him he *had already* bought me a ring. After that revelation, I started wearing the engagement ring, and then the conversations changed.

I was sure that Sam was the perfect man for me, and Daddy's attempts to protect me by culling my boyfriends hadn't worked with him. I was ready to leave home, go to college, and get married. I tried to understand why Daddy was so strict with me. I think, because I was the oldest of four girls, it was probably very hard for him to let go, to see me grow up, and for the first time, have to give up one of his little girls. To him, I may have still been his little Pitty Pat.

We all finally compromised. I would go to Lipscomb for one semester (actually, Lipscomb was on the quarter system), and if Sam and I still wanted to get married after the quarter ended in December, Daddy said he would give us his blessing. He would then sign for me, which would be needed for a seventeen-year-old to marry.

I left for Lipscomb. Daddy let me stop by Sam's house to tell him goodbye, and then he took me on to Nashville. It was a very sad day! I was leaving for college engaged, knowing how much Sam and I would miss each other.

I started classes and really enjoyed college classes. I had always enjoyed school and classes and learning new things—and still do! My part-time job while there was working in the audiovisual department on campus. Although so outdated now, my job was to deliver and pick up film reels used by various professors, department heads, and administrators.

I met a lot of nice people as I went from building to building on campus, delivering films to the professors, the dean, or other administrators. Most of the faculty members were nice enough to stop for a few minutes to talk with me if they had time. I remember one particularly encouraging conversation I had with the dean when I told him I was getting married and would not be back for the next quarter after Christmas. He had always been especially nice to me when I saw him, and he was loved and respected by everyone.

Sam came down to see me every Wednesday and then would often come down on the weekends to bring me back home. He was counting on the fact that we could get married in December when our joint agreement with Daddy had ended. After a few weeks passed, he, in fact, said as much. He said that we would get married in December or not at all!

I had a difficult choice to make. I loved college, but I also loved Sam, and I understood that he was probably tired of driving back and forth to see me.

At an older age, I might have thought more about feeling pressured to make a decision, but in all fairness, I had never discussed my feelings with Sam. He was going to be the breadwinner in our relationship, and I thought his opinions should be the dominant ones.

I was in love! Sam had a good personality, I enjoyed being with him, he had a good job, everyone liked him, and—very important to me—he was a Christian. He had been baptized during a gospel meeting during the summer while we were going together.

I had made an important choice! I was now planning a December wedding. Sam and I got married on December 19, 1960, in Clarkson, Kentucky, at the local Church of Christ where we had met several months before.

Anticipating beginning married life, and the newly increased financial responsibilities that it would entail, Sam traded his red Impala convertible for a Volkswagen Beetle. We drove it from the church after the wedding and stopped to eat our first married meal together at a Frisch's Big Boy in Louisville, Kentucky.

After spending several hours at a local garage the next morning, getting rocks out of the hubcaps, we drove on to Cincinnati, Ohio, for our honeymoon. We stayed only two days as it was snowing very hard. Sam was thinking he needed to get back to work and not get stuck in the snow, so we started back to begin our lives together in our little two-bedroom house on Lilac Road. It was a very happy time!

Sam continued his work at the bank, and I was very happy just staying home and being a homemaker. I cooked and cleaned and took care of everything at home, and Sam even came home from work every day for lunch. We spent as much time as we could together, and going to church together was a big part of that.

When we got married, we were young, but I was convinced that Sam had a good enough job that I wouldn't really need to have a college education or ever need to have a job myself. I was feeling loved, I was now a wife, and I was convinced that Sam would always be able to take care of me and make me happy.

Blinded by love, and in my limited knowledge and experience at the time, I know now that it was not his job to make me happy. At best, he could only *add* to my happiness. I needed to feel secure within myself. Little did I recognize at the time, but I had a lot of insecurities and still had a lot of growing up to do.

I had not learned how to effectively communicate my feelings in a loving and caring manner, and I was afraid that if I didn't marry him when he wanted me to, he would find someone else. There was very little honest communication between the two of us.

I *did* love him, and it was as if being in love was the only thing that mattered, and I believed that how we were feeling then would never change. We had never really talked about our plans for the future, our expectations for each other, or the deepest desires of our hearts. Without that communication, our relationship was doomed for problems, which subsequently came for us both.

So was it a *good choice* to get married so young?

Looking back, and even recognizing all the areas where we both had a lot of growing and learning to do, and even with all our shortcomings, difficulties, disagreements, and eventual parting, I would still say *yes*! To me, the good outweighed the bad! First and foremost, we had three wonderful sons together, and later, grandchildren and great-grandchildren, which has resulted in so much love and enjoyment for me, and which will last for as long as I live.

EIGHT

Early Marriage

When I got married, I had a fairy-tale belief as to what my life would be like. I would get married and live happily ever after. I pictured myself as the consummate homemaker who would have a nice house, be a good housekeeper, and—along with my husband—be respected in the community. I would be a good wife to my husband in every way. I would have children with him, and I would be a good mother to our children and would raise them in a happy home where we all did things together as a family. We would enjoy our times and experiences together; watch our children grow into godly, upstanding citizens; see them happily married; and ourselves fall more in love in our old age. We would then die, leaving behind children and grandchildren who would carry on with their lives while perpetuating a part of ours.

The first few months of my marriage were the fairy tale I had imagined. We were so much in love, and we were happy together. Sam had a good job at the local bank and was poised to become a successful businessman. I had quit college to get married, thinking he would take care of me for the rest of my life, and thinking I wouldn't need to go to college myself. I was convinced that he could make enough money for us to live on, and I could envision being at home and taking care of the house and supporting him in all our joint priorities and endeavors.

I tried to do everything I thought my husband wanted me to do. I became a good cook, kept a tidy house, washed and ironed his clothes, and even ironed his underwear, just like his mother had done. At first, we lived in a little rented two-bedroom house on Lilac Road in Leitchfield, Kentucky, which I thought was totally great!

I immersed myself into being the kind of wife that I thought Sam needed and wanted me to be. I was being the wife that I had always dreamed of being. Sam was the center of attention for me, and my entire being revolved around trying to please him and make him happy as we began to build our lives together.

A few months into our marriage, Sam told me about a job he thought I should apply for as a secretary at the county extension office. Even though I did not especially want the job, I went for an interview and got the job. I was happy being a homemaker, but I had applied for it to make Sam happy, and to help with the finances. Sam had just received a promotion at the bank, and we were hopefully set to be one of the promising young couples in the community. Since our marriage, he had been coming home for lunch, but after getting the job, instead of him coming home for lunch every day, we went out together in town to eat lunch. We enjoyed socializing with other local businesspeople in town, making new friends, and trying to cultivate business contacts for him at the bank. All his customers loved him, and especially the little old ladies. They would often wait in line for several minutes to go to his window where he could wait on them.

It did not cross my mind that we would not live happily ever after. After all, we were both Christians, we went to church together regularly, and Sam even did some fill-in preaching on occasion. We were both from good families, we were both respected and liked, and we had waited until after we were married to consummate our union. We had supposedly done all the right things, as I had been taught to think and believe.

Approximately six months after we were married, we were in church one Sunday morning and had just stood up for what we called the invitation song. I wasn't feeling very well, so I told Sam that I was going to go out and sit in the car and that he could come out to the car after the service had concluded. A few minutes later, he came out, along with quite a few other church members, to find that I had fainted and was laying on the ground in the churchyard. It turned out to be nothing serious, just a natural part of being pregnant—which, at the time, neither he nor I realized. However, we then had just announced to the entire church congregation that I was pregnant.

Sam was so attentive and supportive that Sunday afternoon. I remember feeling nauseated, and going home and laying on the couch with my head in his lap while he put cold washcloths on my forehead. As bad as I felt, I was very happy. We were going to be parents, and that was just the next part of my fairy tale.

During my pregnancy, reality began to set in. I was so very sick during the first months. I continued to work, but I was miserable. The extension office, where I worked as the office secretary, was in the old courthouse at the time, and on many occasions, I would barely make it to the bathroom to vomit. To make matters worse, the bathrooms in the courthouse basement were so unsanitary, they could make any person— pregnant or not—feel nauseated.

I tried to do my job the best I could under the circumstances, and at first, I tried not to let my supervisors know that I was pregnant. I had remembered when I was being interviewed for the job that one of the men had made the statement that he thought I was the best job applicant, but the problem he had with hiring young girls was that, just about as soon as you get them trained and everything is going well, they get pregnant, and you have to start all over again. Even though that might be a true statement, today that would be considered a very discriminatory remark.

Sure enough, I had gotten pregnant very shortly after I had been hired. I was able to hide my condition from the people at the office for a few months, by politely excusing myself to go to the bathroom when I began to feel sick. In those first few months of pregnancy, I remember one day when I was sent across the street to a local hardware store to get some office supplies, and while I was crossing the street, I began to feel dizzy. I thought I was going to faint, but I made it into the store just in time, squatted down, and put my head between my legs, trying to look like I was getting something from a bottom shelf. Thankfully, the queasy feeling passed after a few seconds, and I was able to get the supplies and go back to the office without fainting.

I'm sure everyone in the office would have been supportive, if only I had been open and honest with them in those first few months, but I just couldn't bring myself to tell them after remembering what had been said during the interview. However, it soon became obvious to everyone, and I continued working there several more months until shortly before Alan, my oldest son, was born.

With a little one on the way, other family changes were coming as well. In 1961, we bought our first house, which was located a short distance from town. It was a little, three-bedroom house with a carport, and it cost $9,600, which is hard to believe, considering today's prices. We also had just traded the Volkswagen Beetle for a little Chevy II. Sam made all the business decisions, and I never questioned anything he did, including his selection of the house and car. He made the money, so he was in control of the finances. When we needed something, if he thought we needed it, and if we could afford it, he bought it. It was usually his idea to get new things, rather than mine, such as when he traded our old black-and-white TV for a color TV. He knew when we had enough money to buy new things. I considered Sam as the head of the household, and I viewed my role as the supportive wife who would help to support the choices he made for the two of us.

We never discussed our different roles and contributions to the family as to the importance of each, as I now believe we should have done. Whether as the primary breadwinner or the supportive wife, the value and importance of each should have been weighed and discussed by the two of us.

NINE

Growing Family of Three Boys

My life changed in March 1962 when Alan was born. I became a mother for the first time. Taking care of him became an awesome responsibility, which I embraced with joy. With what I knew as a nineteen-year-old about raising a baby, I used to think Alan was kinda like an experiment.

Alan was born in March 1962, just at the time when most Grayson County sports fans were following Caneyville High School when their team was playing in the state basketball tournament. I was hoping they would win. If I remember correctly, Caneyville defeated Fulton and Henry Clay, and then lost to Ashland. After Alan was born, all the people in the delivery room were having a good time kidding me. They said the first thing I said after I came out from under the anesthetic was, "Did Caneyville win the ball game?" Regretfully, Caneyville did not win, but it was still a happy day for me, as I now had a beautiful baby boy!

Alan was to me the most beautiful baby I had ever seen. I played with him, held him, dressed him up, combed his hair, and loved showing him off. I thought he was just the most adorable little baby in the world. Being the first grandchild on my side of the family, he was always the center of their attention and was doted on by all my family members, including my siblings and grandparents. We all just knew he was the smartest baby ever. When we got together for Sunday dinners at Mama and Daddy's house, he would put on a show! Everyone loved trying to get him to talk. One of his favorite things to say was Madame Chiang Kai-shck. He would say it over and over, as everyone laughed and clapped. For a long time, Alan was our Sunday entertainment!

Sam and I were so proud of Alan, and for many months, we took him everywhere we went. When he was only four months old, we took him with us on a Western vacation. We took the mattress from his crib, put it across the back seat of the Chevy II, and headed for California. One of us could lay across the back seat on the mattress with Alan, and play with him and sleep with him, if needed. By necessity, we also took a diaper pail, which we put in the back floorboard behind the front seat, as we had no disposable diapers at that time. I cannot imagine anyone even thinking about taking a trip like that now.

We had a little scare a few days into the vacation. While we were sightseeing in and around Yellowstone Park, Alan got sick, and we took him to a doctor there. The doctor gave us some medicine for congestion and cold and tried to assure us that he would be OK, so we continued on to California. We stayed there with relatives for a few days and enjoyed sightseeing around San Francisco and Los Angeles. Remarkably, after going on a cruise to Catalina Island one day, Alan's congestion seemed to be gone. We were told that the sea air might have been good for him.

Sam would often take Alan with him on Saturday mornings when he went to a local restaurant to socialize with the guys. Alan loved bacon, and as he was learning to talk, he called it "mundo." All the guys thought that was cute, especially one of the guys who was always at the restaurant and who used to tease him about it as he got older. This was the same person who always told me how bad my coffee was—and I'm sure he was right! He and Sam were both members of the hospital board, and on hospital board nights, he would often ride out to the house with Sam. Sam would hurriedly eat and change clothes, while his friend drank my awful coffee. Then they would leave and go back to a hospital board meeting together.

Several months after Alan was born, I can remember Sam once saying to me that I didn't pay attention to him or do things for him like I used to before we'd had a baby. In all honesty, I guess I didn't. He and the baby had to share my time now. I had traded ironing shorts and socks for changing and washing diapers and taking care of the baby. In retrospect, even with our new baby, we should have made some special time just for each other, such as date nights out together.

We should have also discussed how a baby would change our lives. There were three of us now. There was another person to love, which would take some of the time and attention away from each other, even while adding a new and wonderful dimension to our lives. I wanted to be both a good wife and a good mother, and I wanted Sam to better understand how much time and attention a baby required. I didn't want him to feel neglected because of the time I was spending with our new baby, but I may not have effectively communicated that to him. Effective and honest communication continued to be a weakness in our relationship. I wish we could have been better at that!

After a few months of living in our new house, and now having a new baby, Sam was again talking about me getting a job, like a lot of other women who had babies. Even though I was happy being a wife and full-time mother, I remember thinking maybe I really wasn't doing enough to help out with the finances. After all, my neighbor had a child, and she was working and seemed to be managing quite well.

I had a difficult choice to make: remaining as a full-time mother or trying to help with some of the finances.

Alan was about eighteen months old when I was contacted by one of the local school officials to see if I was interested in doing some substitute teaching. I had left Lipscomb University to get married, and I had ten and two-thirds semester hours that would transfer to Western Kentucky University. I was told I would be teaching with an emergency certificate and would only need six semester hours per year to renew it, since teachers were so desperately needed at that time.

I agreed to do some substitute teaching, thinking I could add a little to our family income and still be at home with Alan a big part of the time. So I enrolled in a Saturday class and was ready to start as a substitute teacher whenever I was called.

My first day of teaching was the day President Kennedy was assassinated, on November 22, 1963. That was a day to remember! I was teaching in a first-grade classroom at the old Leitchfield school building when a fellow teacher across the hall came to tell me the news. Seeing the flag lowered to half-mast, trying to explain what had happened to first graders, and being in a state of shock myself, I wasn't sure I ever wanted to go back into a classroom again after that terrible day. But I did!

Having a young baby, and going back to college in order to work part time, involved a lot of additional work and responsibility on my part. I took a Saturday class each semester and also began taking correspondence courses which I could work on when I was at home with Alan. I took enough correspondence courses to equate to more than a year's credit toward my bachelor's degree.

For several years, I continued to do substitute teaching when I could arrange childcare, sometimes teaching a day or days at a time, a week at a time, or even an entire semester, on a few occasions. By now, I was determined to finish my degree, no matter how long it took. I remember thinking that, as a substitute teacher, I was working just as hard as a certified teacher worked, but I didn't get paid nearly as much. In fact, I only received ten dollars per day as a substitute teacher, but I paid six dollars per day for a babysitter, so that wasn't really very profitable.

I found that I *loved teaching* when I could be in a classroom for an extended period of time, but I did not especially like going in for one day at a time at the last minute. It was especially difficult when no good lesson plans were left for me as the substitute teacher. I *do* know that, in later years, lesson plan requirements definitely improved, which was a positive for substitute teachers. For several years, I had many interesting experiences as a substitute teacher at all levels from elementary to high school.

The hardest time I had as a substitute teacher was when I taught a semester of high school chemistry at Clarkson High School in Clarkson, Kentucky, where I had graduated a few years earlier. I'm not sure how much teaching I really did, but I worked hard at preparing for that class, and I had to study every night. Two of the most interesting days of my substitute teaching career were in a high school agriculture class at Clarkson. The topic being discussed at the time was artificial breeding. Surprisingly, I was very comfortable with that topic as the information was familiar to me since I had grown up on a farm and had been around animals.

Just before Barry, my second son, was born in 1965, we moved to the farm about five miles out of town, where all the boys grew up and lived until graduating from high school and leaving home. We bought the seventy-six-acre farm on Highway 259 South and spent eighteen thousand dollars to build a new house there.

When Barry was born in 1965, my heart grew! While pregnant with him, I remember feeling guilty, thinking I could not possibly love another baby as much as I loved Alan. Boy, was I wrong! I only had to look at that little face, and I knew that it *is* possible to love more than one child, and to love one just as much as the other.

Not that any parent loves a second or third child less than the first, but the initial newness of having a child makes a first child different. With more than one child, as the busyness increases, time restraints also come into play. For example, without a very intentional effort, many of us probably don't have as many photos of our second or third children as we do of the first, even though we love each and every one of them the same.

Barry was an active child, moving so fast at times that he quite often had a bump on his head. He was usually so busy that it was hard to keep up with him. Alan had been so much calmer, and when Barry came along, I jokingly would say, "What have I done?" For a while, I referred to him as my wild child! The two boys were so very different in so many ways, but I soon learned to enjoy their unique personalities and differences.

While at home with the two of them, I tried a few business ventures on my own to try to make some extra money to buy items for our new house on our new farm. I tried selling Pennyrich bras, where I would go to homes and do individual fittings. That endeavor didn't last very long.

We had the land, so I tried raising cucumbers one year when Barry was little, leaving him in his playpen under a shade tree while I picked the cucumbers in the nearby cucumber patch. I knew raising cucumbers was hard work, as that was something we had done years before on the family farm in Big Clifty. I guess I had forgotten just how hard the work would be in the hot summer sun, because as soon as I had recovered all my expenses from the cucumber crop, I just stopped picking the cucumbers and let the cucumber patch grow up in weeds. I decided I didn't need anything else for our new house after all—at least, not that badly!

At our new house on the farm, our living room stayed empty for six years until we were in a position to furnish it. We basically bought new items as we could afford them. I tried to help by buying old pieces of furniture, or taking something that had been given to me and painting or refinishing the item to use in the house. Actually, it didn't really matter that we had an empty room since we also had a family room. That empty room just gave the boys a big space in which to play.

It wasn't long until Barry settled down a little, and then he and Alan were entertaining themselves more often. Now that they were older and were playing well together, I could watch them as they played, and I felt like then I had a little more time for myself.

I continued to take college classes and continued to do some substitute teaching when I could arrange for a babysitter. Sam was continuing to work hard and was becoming more and more involved in business and civic affairs. He was busy working long hours and was gone from home to attend meetings on many nights. Even though he was very busy with work, I sometimes felt like he wasn't doing enough to support *my* efforts as I was working toward getting a teaching certificate, doing substitute teaching, and more importantly, trying to take care of our boys.

The year 1968 was definitely a trying one for our marriage. Without going into all the soap opera details, he and I continued on together. Circumstances improved, and Sam and I tried to work through the difficulties.

In 1969, Sam and I had a third son. Cary was born, and my heart grew even bigger! I now had three sons to love. Cary was such a sweet baby. Many people thought he looked just like Sam when he was little. He was a mixture of Alan and Barry as to his disposition, and when he was born, his older brothers adored him. They helped so much in caring for him and playing with him as he grew, even though he might have "pestered" (I think that was their word) them at times.

My mother-in-law was a big help and support to me during those years by keeping the boys at times while I went to night class, either at Western Kentucky University or to a satellite location as I continued to pursue getting a teaching certificate. I wasn't as comfortable leaving the boys with other people, but on some occasions, I felt I had no other choice. Then, whenever the boys weren't happy about that, I ended up feeling guilty.

During these early years on the farm, we spent a lot of time with Sam's brother and his wife, who lived nearby. Being a young wife and mother, I learned so many things from my sister-in-law. I thought she could do anything, and I wanted to be just as good a homemaker as I perceived her to be. Among her many talents were cooking, sewing, crafts, and decorating. I admired all her domestic skills. We spent a lot of time cooking together, canning together, and freezing vegetables and fruit together. We often took turns cooking meals and eating together with our families, and sometimes, our families all went different places together. I have so many fond memories of the times our families spent together when all our children were younger.

Cary was the baby of the family, and Alan and Barry thought I was easier on him than I had been with them. As I think back, there was probably some truth to their accusations. I think, when I became so involved and engrossed with some of my own personal problems, I may have let things go with him, and I may have let him get by with behaviors which I had handled differently with the two of them. Another consideration was evident. As I had gotten older and busier, I progressively had less energy, and probably just out of being so tired, I had let some things go instead of following through at times.

To me, having three children was ideal. With two, I could see how one child could possibly be the mother's favorite and the other the father's favorite, but with three, there would be less chance of a favorite for either of us. I felt I could better look at each of my three boys as a unique individual, and I could realize just how special he was in his own individual way.

I remember the thought once crossed my mind (and maybe I even jokingly said) that it might be nice if parents could just take a little bit of a particular characteristic from one child and give it to another one, but I knew that was not really possible. I *was*—and *am*—thankful that God made all my sons different, as each has his own endearing charms which makes him so very special! I learned to cherish their differences. I believe *all* children are gifts from God, just as I considered each of *my own* children to be a gift from God.

With such differences in personalities and interests, there was always something fun or interesting going on for me to enjoy. I never wanted to compare my children as to their individual abilities, and I hoped they would not compare themselves with each other. Each had his own special gifts and abilities and was a unique individual in his own right. I also believed this to be true in regard to teaching my students.

I have always enjoyed being around young children. I think that is why I spent most of my teaching years at the first-grade level. I loved my little first graders. I loved their honesty, their innocence, their sense of enjoyment, and their excitement at the simple pleasures of life.

When I had a concern or had something on my mind, I found that my first graders, as well as my own children, had a way of making me focus on what was really important. One thing that was so refreshing about being around children was that they could always make me forget about any of my own perceived problems or concerns while I was with them or interacting with them. Just something as simple as a hug from a child could always brighten my day!

Most teachers have a preference for students at certain grade levels, just as parents may enjoy their own children more at different ages. And that's OK! Dealing with the normal behaviors of younger children sometimes requires a lot of patience. However, some of the innocent, mischievous little actions (not the mean or hurtful ones) of young children were qualities I always enjoyed about working with the younger ones. That made teaching first graders fun for me!

Another reason I liked teaching first grade had to do with my personal philosophy of teaching: prevention versus remediation. Teaching reading was what I loved to do! It was a lot more fun and more productive to try to prevent problems, trying to give children a good start by building a good foundation for learning, rather than trying to do remedial work at a later date. It was so rewarding for me to see a child's eyes light up when he realized he could actually read! Today, many children learn to read earlier than first grade, but there are still challenges for some, just as there were when I was teaching.

In actuality, that same philosophy could prove to be very relevant in many other areas. It's far more productive and rewarding to spend time teaching children at each stage of development, rather than trying to solve problems later. The key is spending the time!

As well as enjoying the children in my classes at school, I likewise enjoyed all three of my own children as they were growing and learning. I enjoyed their little antics, which were often humorous and entertaining to me. There were so many I remember, but I will share just one example for each son that comes to mind.

Back in 1964, when Alan was just a little over two years old, we went to the New York World's Fair, taking my sister Brenda with us. We later decided to go to Canada and had to cross the border to get to Niagara Falls. Alan had begged for something to drink, seemingly for many miles, but Sam kept on driving, telling him we would be stopping soon and he could get a drink when we stopped. When we got to the border crossing, we were stopped by the authorities. They were asking for information such as where we were from, where we were going, and what we wanted to see and do in Canada. Alan was in the back seat with the window rolled down, listening to the conversation, when all of a sudden he shouted out, "Hey, man! I'm from Leitchfield, 'Tucky, and I just want a drink of water." We all laughed, including the border authorities, and it wasn't much longer before Alan got his drink of water!

The boys each had a lot of varied interests and were always going from one activity to another. One day, Barry was playing with his little cars and airplanes in the family room. I looked up and saw he had stretched toilet paper all the way from the bathroom, down the long hallway, and into the family room. When I saw it, I said, "Barry Neal, what do you think you are doing?" To which he innocently looked up and, as a matter of fact, said, "I'm making a runway for my airplanes." I just had to laugh, and I thought that actually was really smart and imaginative. So I just let him go on playing until he had wasted the entire roll. He continued playing for quite some time with that toilet paper runway.

Occasionally, we would go out to eat in our hometown of Leitchfield, Kentucky. We sometimes went to one of the few nicer local restaurants. One night, we had finished enjoying a meal together and were on our way to the car when Cary came running after us. He was jumping up and down and was so excited, and with his little outstretched hand, he loudly said, "Daddy, Daddy! Here, Daddy, you left your money on the table!" I guess Cary either didn't think our waitress deserved a tip, or maybe that was in some way the beginning of his conservative thinking.

During their middle school and high school years, each of the boys were given nicknames by certain friends that stuck with them for years. Alan was known as Alpo. Barry was known as Melba. Cary was known as Neuk. If someone around town was talking about someone known by one of those names, many people would know exactly to whom they were referring. Many friends had a lot of fun using those names.

While living on the farm, the boys all became more and more involved in school and sports activities—mainly baseball, football, basketball, and golf. Their interests seemed to change with every season. We continued to go to church on Sunday mornings, Sunday nights, and Wednesday nights.

Many Sundays after church, it was a race after we got home to see who got the couch first to watch Sunday afternoon ball games.

The boys' interests became much more narrow as they entered high school. At that point, most of their activities centered around basketball and golf. They spent many hours representing the Grayson County High School teams. When not in a school activity, they might be found playing basketball at home in the driveway or at a friend's house, or playing golf at the golf course which was within walking distance of where we lived. If they wanted to, I'm sure each of my three boys could probably write a book about all their own high school sports activities and memories.

The farm was a good place to raise three boys. They had a big yard in which to play. It was big enough for a friendly baseball game or for hitting golf balls, even though a ball would occasionally go astray and end up hitting the house or a window. There was a basketball goal in the driveway where many hours were spent shooting, dribbling, and scoring. There was a pond for fishing, and the pond's depth was a source of many discussions among the boys, and especially with one special friend who was often at our house.

At night, Cary and his cousin who lived nearby, or another friend, would often go gigging for frogs. They would clean the frogs and bring them to me so I could cook the frog legs. Although they might have "jumped" around in the skillet while cooking, the frog legs were good eating!

On the farm, there were also acres of woods in which to hunt, or to just go out and explore with friends. There was room on the farm to run and play with a dog. We essentially had two dogs while the boys were growing up on the farm. I have specific memories of each. Bounce was the first. Sam traded a record player to a friend for Bounce, a big, beautiful collie. Alan and Barry did a lot of running and playing out in the yard with Bounce.

The days when the school bus stopped out front on the highway, Bounce might follow Alan out to the highway near where the bus would stop, and where he would sometimes stay and bark at the cars. Sometimes, I had to go get Bounce to bring him back to the house. He often would follow us when we were in the car and driving out to the highway to go somewhere, and then he would stay there for a while, barking at all the cars that passed.

One day, in his excitement at barking at all the cars, Bounce got hit by a car. The boys and I saw what had happened, and we ran out to the road. I drove the car out there, and we gently loaded him into the trunk of the car and took him to the vet. Unfortunately, he did not survive! We reluctantly brought him home and had a "dog funeral" for our beloved pet and buried him out in the barnyard next to the fence. That was a sad time for the boys and me!

A few years later, another dog came into the picture. A stray dog wandered onto our property, and Cary "took up" with the stray dog. That dog was far from normal! But we kept him around! He had this habit of turning over on his back, with his legs in the air, when someone new came by. That proved to be a lot of fun for my daddy when he came by to visit. Daddy would always rub the dog's tummy when he turned upside down. We named the dog Digger, since he loved to dig! As soon as I would put plants in the flower bed or in pots on the patio, the next time I would look, there would be dirt and plants all over the patio. Digger had been up to no good!

But digging wasn't as bad as the dog's other habit. His worst habit was that he would *not* go to the grass to do his "business." We would find that Digger had used the brick patio instead, and I was usually the one who had to wash off the patio every day. After this went on for a while, I was really getting frustrated as I was the one who did practically all of the cleaning. One night, I said in frustration, "I don't have time to wash off this patio every day! If that dog 'goes' on the patio one more time, we're getting rid of him!"

Early the next morning, as we were finishing breakfast and getting ready to go to school, I looked out on the patio, and there was Cary with a shovel. Sure enough, Digger had done it again! Cary was cleaning up the dog's doodoo himself because he thought I would be getting rid of Digger if I saw it. After seeing Cary out there, and thinking about Cary being out there cleaning off the patio before he went to school, I rethought the situation. I thought, if he loved that dog that much, maybe we should just keep him. So we did! Digger was still frustrating, but we kept him for a long time, and we continued to clean up his messes—until one day he disappeared! What happened to him is another story!

We had cattle on the farm, and my father-in-law was frequently around to check on the animals. Occasionally, I would help him with some farm-related tasks when no one else was around to help. I especially remember one day when he asked me to come out to the field with him to help him "pull a calf" from a cow that was having trouble giving birth. That turned out to be quite an experience, even for a farm girl like me! I had never seen that happen when I was growing up on the farm at home.

One Sunday afternoon, when I thought I saw my father-in-law there at the house and farm checking on the cattle, it turned out to be something quite different. We all loved him, but Papaw Woody was a different breed! Sometimes, he would come over to the house and would just stand at the back patio door, looking inside and watching the kids, but never saying a word, and not wanting to come in. He would just stand there, looking inside the house, and would smile at us. It really didn't bother us, and we were used to seeing him standing outside but not usually wanting to come inside.

That particular Sunday afternoon, I had just received a call from my sister-in-law, who lived right down the road. She asked me if I had heard that four convicts had escaped from the state penitentiary near Eddyville, and that they had been spotted near Bear Creek, which was near where we both lived. I told her I had not heard, but that the kids and I were home by ourselves. Sam had gone to Cincinnati to a Bengals football game, and I wasn't expecting him to be home before dark. I was concerned and did not want to stay at home with the boys by myself.

I had a choice to make. Do I stay home, or do I try to leave? I decided to leave! I told my sister-in-law that I was going to get ready and would come to their house.

My car was parked outside, so I hurriedly ran out to get it. I pulled it inside the garage, put down the garage door, and quickly got coats on the boys. I was getting ready to put the kids in the car and leave to go to my brother and sister-in-law's house. After I got their coats on and was getting ready to go to the garage, I looked out the back sliding door, where I saw a man standing on the patio and looking toward the door. I thought it was my father-in-law who had probably come over to check on the cattle and was just standing there and looking inside, as we were used to seeing him do.

All of a sudden, he started running. I looked out and saw him hurriedly climb over the fence. A few seconds later, I saw him lying face down out in the field not far from the garage.

I was scared! I was thinking about the escaped convicts! I told the kids to duck down behind the couch while I ran to the phone and called the police. I told the police I thought the escaped convicts were somewhere around my house, and I thought they had just shot my father-in-law and that he was now lying face down and immobile in the field next to the house.

In the next few minutes, the police were at my door and there was a helicopter buzzing around overhead. It turned out that the police had been across the road from my house and had spotted one of the convicts from the helicopter. That man lying in my field—who had a few minutes before been at my back door—was *not* my father-in-law, but was one of the convicts who had actually surrendered to the police. He had surrendered and was now lying there on the ground with his hands over his head. It was such a relief when I learned it had not been my father-in-law after all, but I was still frightened that the convict had been so close to my back door.

That next few days were very scary for those of us living in that area, as three of the convicts were still on the loose, one of whom had relatives in the area. Later, when Sam got home, we decided to leave the car outside at night *with the keys in it*. Our thinking was that, if they came back, they hopefully would just take the car and leave. We put all the boys with us in our bedroom at night, and we lined up furniture all down the hallway so we could hear any intruder if they tried to advance to our room, and Sam kept a loaded gun beside our bed.

The next day at school, a mother of one of my first graders came running into the classroom to get her son, who was one of my students at the time. She was obviously very shaken! One of the other three escaped convicts had made it across the "holler" and had been to her house and had held her and her baby hostage until her husband came home for lunch. He then took their car and left. In an effort to protect her little ones, that "mama bear" wanted *all* her little ones with her, and she had come to my classroom to get her first grader.

Sometime later, after the other two convicts were in custody, Sam decided he would unload the gun and put it away. Thinking he had all the ammunition out, and instead of going outside, he just pointed the gun down toward the floor in the family room and pulled the trigger. I heard the shot and went running from the back bedroom to the family room to see him standing there above a big hole in the family room floor. Unbelievable!

The episode of the escaped convicts caused a lot of excitement at our house and in the neighborhood for quite some time, and needless to say, it has been one of my *most told* stories!

Sam was a good provider for the boys and me, and he deserves much credit for that. We had every material thing we needed, but we saw less and less of him as he became more and more involved in the many activities that he deemed to be important to his success as a banker. He was going to many meetings with what I termed "big shots," and he was spending a lot of time with them. This worried me, and I expressed my concerns as many of them did not seem to share the same values and beliefs that I thought we both shared.

When Sam had to work late and had a meeting that same evening, and when he felt like he didn't have time to come home before the meeting, I often packed up the kids and took his supper to the bank. That way, they could see him at least for a few minutes.

I mopped floors when we owned a laundromat, I stuffed newspapers when we were part owners of a newspaper, and I did cleaning when we owned an apartment building—and during many of these times, I took the kids with me.

In many years while the boys were growing up, we did all have many nice family times together. There were fun Christmases at home, playing in the yard together or out on the farm, and we enjoyed some wonderful vacation trips together. We took Sam's mother and daddy on vacation with us one year, and we took *my* mother and daddy on vacation with us another year. I was also able to enjoy several trips with Sam because of his position at the bank, which otherwise I might never have experienced. We went to Hawaii together two different times, went with friends to Puerto Rico, went with friends to Paris, as well as several other places.

As Sam immersed himself into his work and community and civic activities, he continued to get promotions and pay raises. He was so engrossed in his work that he had little time left to help around the house or with the kids, so it was up to me to see that the boys and the home were taken care of in all ways.

As the kids got older and became more deeply involved in their own activities, I didn't feel like I could continue to be gone so much with Sam by accompanying him to so many meetings without making the boys miss out on school and childhood activities with friends. I spent a lot of time taking the boys to sports practices and games, and I enjoyed being there myself to watch them as they participated.

Along with their friends, they all three wanted to be involved in many different activities, and in order for them to participate, I needed to be available to provide the transportation and coordinate all their schedules. That lasted until they became drivers themselves. As the three boys depended on me more and more, and I couldn't arrange to accompany Sam as often on bank trips and outings, he would more often go without me.

I felt like I was trying to support Sam as best I could, and I went with him to civic meetings or on bank trips when I could arrange it. Many times, I *would* have gone, but could not get a babysitter. I didn't want to disappoint the boys, and I wanted to go with Sam. At those times, I wished I could do both! I hoped he would understand and appreciate that I was trying to be a good mother as well as a supportive wife.

Sam was becoming so busy and involved in so many different pursuits, he was seldom at home in the evenings, was missing out on going to church with us, and was often gone for days at a time. I wanted to think that his family was as important to him as it was to me. I knew he worked hard, but I hoped he would find a way to work less and spend more time with us. I wanted it to be a priority to him to spend more time with us.

I felt such enormous responsibility for the boys in all areas, from church attendance and educational activities to social outings, family activities, and all their own individual sports activities. Besides just making money, I wanted Sam to feel some of that responsibility as well, as I felt I was also working hard. It seemed to me as if he didn't have to worry about me taking care of our family when he was gone, when he knew I would be there with them.

The years 1974 to 1975 was another time of crisis for us. Again, without all the soap opera details, we stayed together.

Shortly thereafter, it was decided that we would make an addition to our house on the farm. We had a basement dug out under the original house, did some remodeling, and built an addition onto the back of the house. The addition cost ninety thousand dollars in 1976, when the original house had been built for eighteen thousand dollars in 1965.

The best thing about that addition was that, now that the boys were older, they had the entire basement to entertain their friends. For most of their teen years, we took advantage of that. I liked having my kids at home. I didn't worry as much. I enjoyed my boys. I enjoyed their friends, and their friends seemed to like being there, as I often would cook for them or make cookies for all of them.

Many times, when we might be expecting to have snow days at school, a lot of the boys would end up in our basement and would sometimes get snowed in and would be there at our house for a few days at a time. The boys kept busy with their friends and activities. I was busy with them, and when they asked, I began to make excuses as to why their daddy was gone so much.

The more money Sam made, the more he was gone, and the less it seemed he needed me. He could now afford to pay others for what I used to do for him. He could pay someone to do his laundry and iron all his clothes. I used to do all that! He could pay for a pedicure. I used to cut his toenails! He could pay for someone else to pamper him. The kids and I used to "walk" on his back, and he used to lay in my lap while I combed his hair or rubbed his face when he was tired! He could now afford to eat at nice restaurants, which of course, were fancier meals than I had always cooked at home for him every night or which were taken to him at the bank when he was working late.

All these changes made me feel less important. I felt like I was being taken for granted, as I was staying home and doing all the hard lifting with our family while he was traveling to fun places or out enjoying some fancy meal or attending a social activity with friends and colleagues.

When he *was* at home, I usually expressed my displeasure at him being gone so much, which he probably saw as complaining—and maybe it was! I thought all the things I was doing for our family were just as important as making money.

Sam had moved up to be president and CEO of the bank, and I now had a full-time teaching position. With both of us having reached a milestone, it seemed to me the perfect time for us to slow down a little and enjoy more time together as a family, which I thought we could now afford to do, and which I expressed to him quite frequently.

I continued to try to balance work and family. Along with all the home and family responsibilities, I was continuing college classes as I could work them into our busy schedules. By the time I had finally finished my required bachelor's degree and my master's degree with an endorsement as a reading specialist, and had added a Rank 1 degree in educational administration, I had been taking college classes on and off for twenty-four years.

Whenever Sam *was* at home, which was more and more for shorter periods of time, I was usually complaining about how much he was always gone and how he hardly ever spent time with me and the boys. I thought he was working too hard and was gone from home too much. But nothing I said or did seemed to matter!

Looking back, I can understand how Sam might have felt some sense of relief when he was out and doing things with others. At least, he didn't have to listen to my complaints and jealousy about the time spent with others, or my complaining about him being gone so much, rather than being with me and the kids. Even though we all missed him, I felt like he seemed to be enjoying time and activities with others more than being at home with us.

I think maybe I could have handled the situation differently, although I'm not sure what really might have helped. I *do* know, all the complaints did not help! They probably just made things worse!

TEN

Roller-Coaster Years

For years, it seemed I had been fighting for my marriage and for more family time together, and then in 1980, there was another crisis to face, which after three *long* years resulted in my first divorce after twenty-three years of marriage. (Again, without *most* of the soap opera details.)

After years of worry, concern, and questioning, I was feeling increasingly insecure in my marriage relationship. It was becoming more and more difficult for me to continue with our present circumstances and still be able to keep my life on an even keel. I was becoming an emotional wreck!

I do not want to besmirch Sam, as he had many wonderful qualities I loved and still admire. We all sin differently, and like many other people, we had our own individual and personal weaknesses and insecurities. Looking back, I do not believe *initially* that there was an absence of love, but mainly the absence of developing and utilizing effective communication skills in our relationship. This inability to effectively communicate our feelings and insecurities in a loving and caring manner seemed to often result in misunderstandings, arguments, disagreements, disappointments, and questioning.

Before we married, we had never talked about our deep-seated beliefs and hopes for the future. Even though both of us were part of the marriage relationship, I have to individually accept my part of the responsibility for not having had those discussions. Without an open line of honest communication, our relationship was doomed for problems, which subsequently came.

I had grown up in the Church of Christ, and I had heard it preached and taught over and over that you should marry someone who was a member of the church. Sam and I were both members of the church, and at my young age, and with limited knowledge and experience, I naively believed *that alone* would assure that we would have a lifetime of marital bliss. Both of us were Christians, and I thought that would be the primary criterion for my having a happy marriage.

To this day, I still believe that, to have a godly and joyful marriage, it is best to marry a Christian. But I now realize that that is just the beginning point! There were other relationship skills that I could have learned and *should* have learned before I married, but I was like so many other young people in love who rush into a relationship with little thought as to the future.

I can remember thinking when I was younger (and may have even said to classmates and friends of other denominations), that they were going to hell if they didn't go to the Church of Christ.

I am sorry if anyone remembers ever having that conversation with me. Many of my beliefs have been refined! I believe that all who profess Jesus Christ to be the Son of God; who desire with all their heart to be faithful, lifetime followers of Jesus; who have sincerely repented of their sins; and who were baptized in the name of the Father, the Son, and the Holy Spirit for the remission of their sins are forgiven children of God. They are then part of God's family, and they are my sisters and brothers.

I'm very thankful for the spiritual upbringing that I *did* receive during my formative and teenage years. It was good that my parents always took me to church and taught me moral values. However, I did not have a complete understanding of many things I heard in Sunday school and church, and there were very few additional discussions at home. It wasn't until I was older and searched the Scriptures for myself, that I more fully understood some important truths.

Even with all the marital problems that were becoming more evident in my marriage, I did not want a divorce. My belief about marriage was that you should marry *once*, and that the marriage should be for a lifetime. In my situation, even if I believed there were biblical reasons for a divorce, I still did not want a divorce. For a while, I was hopeful that our problems would just blow over, as they had with prior episodes, or that we could finally talk or work out our problems.

Instead, there were more and more complications that were becoming evident, and as a result, this period of my life became like an unpredictable soap opera. For three years, with all the highs and lows I was experiencing, all the curves, and all the ups and downs, I felt like I was on a roller coaster, and I never did like roller coasters!

I wanted to try to salvage my marriage, but considering the deeply difficult circumstances at the time, there seemed to be no mutual interest in trying to do so. For a long time, I held out hope for reconciliation. At first, there were no divorce papers filed. Sam and I were no longer living together, and we hadn't been living together for many months. I kept busy with my teaching and with the boys, continuing to take the boys to all their activities and to church, but I felt like my life was on hold. Until the boys finished high school, I tried to be strong for them. I tried to put on my best face and pour myself into my work and their activities.

There had been no meaningful communication with Sam for over a year. Day by day, my life was becoming more and more in turmoil. Our personal marital situation by now had become increasingly complicated. I was unsure about my future. I knew things might get harder for me, and I somehow needed to find a way to keep my sanity! I didn't see how I could ever get back to a "normal" life, and I increasingly became convinced that I needed to make a difficult choice. That was a time in my life when I just had to run over the skunk!

Since I did not want a divorce, I filed for a legal separation. My thinking was that I would still be married, while trying to salvage enough of the marital assets to take care of our children. If reconciliation ever did occur, then our marital assets could be put back together. For multiple reasons, there was no reconciliation, and sadly, our divorce ultimately became final.

My mother and daddy were a big help to me at this time. Money was scarce and restricted, and it was hard to continue paying the bills for the home where the kids and I were still living. I did not have money for paying some of the bills or for a lawyer, so Daddy wrote me a check for ten thousand dollars. After finally figuring out how to get access to more funds, I later tore up the check that Daddy had written to me. More important than the offer of monetary help from my mother and father was just their *presence*. Almost every day, they would have some reason to stop by my house after I got home from school. I didn't really feel like having company, but they would be there anyway! They wouldn't leave me alone, even though, at that time, I sometimes wished they would.

As I look back, it was good that they made the effort to check on me, and later on, I appreciated my parents even more and got to tell them so. In times of great distress, I learned that sometimes, the best thing you can do for a person is exactly what they did for me—to just be there for me, to just sit with me, to talk if I wanted to, or to just let me know how much they loved me. That was not the time for a lecture or for causing even more guilt! I was truly blessed to have had wonderful, godly parents who supported me during this very trying time of my life.

After three years apart and much adversity, my divorce from Sam became final, and I was now *alone* with the boys. As I realized the finality of the divorce, I was heartbroken! I was devastated! I was humiliated! I felt betrayed! I felt unloved! I felt unappreciated! I was angry! I was disappointed! I was disillusioned with many friends!

There were supposed "friends" of ours who I felt were taking sides, and even though I understood, it was nevertheless disheartening. They were no longer acting as our *mutual* friends, with whom we had enjoyed many good times. I felt abandoned and betrayed! I never actually confronted any of these people or talked to them about my feelings, and I realize now that, for their own reasons, many of them must have felt conflicted. Nevertheless, I felt much anguish and despair! I had to move on without them!

> Things change and friends leave. Life doesn't stop for anybody!
> —Stephen Chbosky

Even after the initial shock of my divorce being final, I still had to deal with all the drama of working and living in a small town with my ex-husband, where everyone knew all the salacious details of our lives. And many times, I had to endure actions being flaunted before my very eyes. I could imagine all the talk and small-town gossip! I know *now* that was mostly a *pride* thing!

I remember thinking afterward that divorce has to be *almost* as devastating as death! Losing a husband or wife you love—*through a divorce you don't want*—could prove to be just as emotionally devastating as losing a spouse in death.

If a beloved spouse dies, grief is shared by family members and friends. There is often a vast support group who all share in the grief, many of whom are blood relatives. Those around the person tend to concentrate on the *good memories* as they try to provide support.

On the other hand, divorce memories are usually not pleasant ones. In a lengthy marriage when couples have been together for so long, have children together, and have intertwined their lives with other family members, there are many more thoughts and emotions that weigh on the heart and mind, so much of which is personal and known only to the grieving spouse. The grieving party shoulders so much hurt, betrayal, rejection, and sorrow that no one else can possibly imagine or comprehend. The closest to that understanding might be someone who has had a similar experience themselves.

The *relationship dies*, but you have to find a way to go on alone, while still seeing and hearing about the departed person. Even though they are dead to you, he or she isn't dead to others. For the grieving person in a divorce, it's often so very hard to let go and accept the finality of the situation. That was certainly true for me!

Hebrews 12:5–8 (NIV) teaches that we should endure hardship as discipline, because God is treating us as a true son, just as an earthly father would discipline his son whom he loved. We are told that if we are not disciplined then we are not true sons. We are illegitimate. We are reminded that God disciplines us for our good, so that we may share in His holiness, and that no discipline seems pleasant at the time, but is painful. But later on, it will produce a harvest of righteousness and peace for those who have been trained by it.

Even though I understand it now, in the midst of my struggles, that passage wasn't really very comforting to me. I can remember thinking when I was so distraught and miserable, *Well, God must love me an awful lot, because I sure am miserable!*

I recognize now that all my misery and unhappiness at the time was part of God's discipline for me, and even then, after that divorce, He wasn't through with me yet! Sad to say, He had a lot more disciplining to do before he *finally* got my attention!

Looking back, there were situations and interactions during those roller-coaster years that I should have handled differently. To say the least, some of my actions were not very Christlike. I have to accept *my* responsibility for those actions and behaviors, as well as my innermost thoughts and feelings of extreme dislike or hatred toward those I felt were the cause of my unhappiness. That includes Sam, as well as any others who were characters in the soap opera.

Even though we divorced, I will always have a loving connection with Sam. If for no other reason, it is through the love we both have for our three sons. Even though none of us in our family has been perfect, I am *proud* of our three sons, especially when I see how they have always treated others—as well as how they have always treated me!

Thankfully, their father and I have made peace with each other and can now converse in a kind and cordial manner.

It may be that, to get back to God, which I believe Sam and I *both* have done, we had to be apart or with others.

I have to trust in God's plan for our lives, even if I do not completely understand it!

Knowing the end of the story doesn't mean you can't cry at the sad parts!
—Mindful Christianity

ELEVEN

Struggling with Beliefs

After my divorce from Sam, I became somewhat disillusioned with church. I started questioning religion. I thought I was trying to do what was right, but my life to that point had not been working out the way I had expected. I continued to take the boys to church as long as they were at home, and if it hadn't been for them, I might have stopped going to church altogether.

I had been taught biblical principles as I had attended church services all during my younger years, and now after a divorce, I was feeling such deep disappointment. During all my growing-up years, going to church was a primary activity for our family. We attended every Sunday morning, Sunday night, and Wednesday night. At one time, we had a Volkswagen, and all of us would cram into that car and ride to church. It was only a few minutes' drive, but with Mama, Daddy, Granny, and all six kids crammed in, it was a very crowded car. Even at that, no one ever complained!

Along with other members, Daddy would sometimes lead the congregational singing. We had no instrumental music in the Church of Christ where we went, but a tuning fork was often used to get the songs started.

We attended a lot of gospel meetings at nearby sister churches where a gospel meeting was being held, and we got to know a lot of the preachers and members in various congregations. Many times, the preacher was invited to our house for Sunday dinner; and sometimes, out-of-town preachers stayed with us in our home when we had a gospel meeting at our own church.

In the earlier years, the church building where we attended at Big

Clifty had no air conditioning, and the meetings were often held in the heat of summer. To keep cool, we used hand fans that were provided by the local funeral homes, and which usually had beautiful religious pictures on them.

It was during one of those gospel meetings that I was baptized, and since we had no baptistry at our little Big Clifty church, we drove to Leitchfield and used the baptistry there. Becoming a Christian was one of the *good choices* of my life! In fact, the *most important choice*!

When we were young, my siblings and I played church a lot. Sitting on the stair steps at our house, one of us would be the preacher, one would lead the singing, and others would pass the crackers and grape juice around for pretend communion.

Going to church was always an important part of growing up in our family, and no one in our house ever said he didn't want to go. We knew that was just what we did, and we were expected to do it as a family, and at the scheduled times, all of us were always ready to go.

Regular church attendance continued through the entire time I lived at home. We changed churches and started going to Clarkson Church of Christ after my siblings and I started going to Clarkson School, where I later graduated. It was there, during my senior year in high school, that I met Sam, who later became the father of my three children.

It was after my divorce from Sam that my idea of what a Christian should be started to evolve. I felt so disappointed and disillusioned at even the thought of no longer being married. Just going to church, and *knowing all the rules* and trying hard to follow them, seemingly hadn't worked for me.

After all I thought I had done in trying to be a good wife and mother, I felt like I was now being cast aside like an old rag. I was feeling sorry for myself and was feeling very defeated. After fighting for so many years and wanting to be happily married, I *had lost*, and I was having a hard time accepting the finality of the situation.

My prideful self had a hard time letting go of the fact that my children's father no longer wanted to be with me. It was so disheartening to think that we had worked at building our lives and fortunes together for over twenty years, and that when we finally *had it made*, that Sam could possibly leave. I kept replaying that over and over in my mind. I don't think

I knew until many years later how that divorce had affected my life and my behaviors for many years to come, including in my subsequent marriages.

During the troubling years of my marriage, and after my divorce became final, I was having many different emotions. I had been part of a couple since I was seventeen years old. I was in somewhat of a financial struggle to ensure the future livelihood of my three children and myself. I felt like an outcast in my church, where I had attended for so many years with Sam and the boys, and where the boys and I were now attending without him. I sometimes felt it was doing me no good at all to keep going to church the way I was feeling, but nevertheless, I continued to go.

I felt like I had very little support in my struggle from friends at church, and I felt like I had been fighting the battle of going through the divorce alone. Even though everyone at church was still nice and polite to me and my children, no one at church ever asked me if they could help in any way. In their defense, I was too *proud* to ask for help! I had heard all the sermons on divorce and how marriage was for life. I believed that myself—and I had prayed a lot that God would save my marriage. I had prayed over and over for a happy marriage and for a restored relationship with Sam, but God had not answered my prayers. So, at that time, I didn't feel like I had much of a connection with God.

In thinking about my future, I found it hard to believe that any man would ever want to start a relationship with a woman who had three teenage sons. I could understand how hard it would be for someone else to accept us all as a package deal, and I felt sure that I was destined to be alone forever!

I soon discovered that someone actually *did* want me. Looking back at that time, I was feeling so unwanted, so unloved, so alone, so undesirable, and so insecure that I married the first person who actually said he wanted to *be with me*. That really wasn't fair to him, and at a later time, I had a chance to talk to him and to apologize and tell him so. He was a good person, he was good to my boys, and—importantly to me at the time—he was someone who thought going to church together was important.

My second marriage definitely was a rebound marriage that lasted less than a year. Almost immediately, I was in disbelief as to the choice I had actually made to get married again so soon! It was hard for me to think that I had made such a mistake. To this day, that marriage seems like a blur. That was *not* one of my better choices!

After making the seemingly thoughtless decision of a rebound marriage, I was determined not to rush into another relationship so quickly. Besides, having been divorced two times, I didn't think that I could ever have another meaningful relationship, anyway. I felt like I was a tainted person whom no decent person would ever want for a wife.

I can see now some of the *godly discipline* that came from the mistake of my second marriage. Making a big, public spectacle of a mistake myself made me begin to think about forgiving others who had wronged me so publicly. The mistakes and sins of others may have been different than mine, but whatever they were, they were each a result of individual weaknesses and sins. I began to think that, if I wanted to be forgiven for *my* mistakes, I had to forgive those who had wronged me. I needed to forgive everyone—all of them! I needed to try to let go of the hurt and anger, and stop feeling sorry for myself, count my blessings, and get on with life.

> For if you forgive other people when they sin against you, your heavenly Father will also forgive you. But if you do not forgive others their sins, your Father will not forgive your sins.
> —Matthew 6:14–15, NIV

During those turbulent years, I had begun to see evidence of what I believed were very Christian acts of *kindness* extended to me which were so much appreciated during this difficult period of my life. I experienced many positive acts of kindness which demonstrated how I felt a Christian brother or sister should be treated in times of difficulty, and some of these kindnesses were now being shown to me.

> No act of kindness, no matter how small is ever wasted.
> —Aesop

Some of the people who became supportive in my life did not go to my church, or maybe didn't go to church at all, but they came to be a source of help in different ways during some trying times. Several showed concern and kindness that I perceived to be truly Christian acts toward someone in need.

There were those who would ask me to go to the basketball games with them, or we would just sit together and enjoy the games when my boys were playing. They didn't discuss my problems or try to take sides, but they were just there *for* me and *with* me many times.

There were those who were so thoughtful as to include me in several outings, or who invited me to go on spring break trips with them when they knew I would probably be left out. There was the one who created special memories for me by filming my boys playing golf and basketball and giving me the tapes. There were friends who vacationed with me and my boys. There were others who arranged or invited me to dinner many times.

There were several at the school where I was teaching who provided friendly encouragement during the three years of my divorce proceedings. There were those who became friends, and still remain as friends, as well as three special friends who have sadly passed away too soon.

There were those who were thoughtful enough to stop by my house to see if I needed anything, or those who would—without my asking—clear my driveway after a big snowfall.

There was my loving brother (who is now deceased) who, as a doctor, always had a heart for people (including me) when he saw hurt and suffering. One day, when I was terribly upset and had stopped and was just sitting in my car on the side of the road in the middle of town, he pulled over beside me. He saw that I was upset and crying, so he got out and walked to my car. He just sat with me for a while and kindly listened and waited with me until I regained my composure.

There were all the young people who were friends of my boys and who came to my house so many times and often ended up enjoying times together in my basement. They all added a lot of much-needed joy to my life.

Through all these many acts of kindness or togetherness, the golden rule began to take on a new meaning to someone such as me, who was in the midst of so many struggles.

Do to others as you would have them do to you.
— Luke 6:31 NIV

Through being the recipient of so many kindnesses, my thinking began to change. I was beginning to more fully realize the difference between the *letter of the law* and the *spirit of the law*, and the difference between *just going to church* and *being the church*. And those were important distinctions for me to learn and to begin to live!

I had always been taken to church and had gone to church—to a church *building*—but I began to more fully realize that the *church* consisted of the *people*—fellow Christians who showed Christlike behaviors toward others in their everyday lives as well as at the church building.

It was during this period of my life when I was feeling like such an outcast, and so tainted by divorce, that once again, when I really did not feel like going to a church service, I made a good choice and went to a church building anyway! The Christian minister that day spoke on a passage from Luke 7:36–47 (NIV).

He spoke of Jesus being anointed by a woman who had lived a sinful life. I felt a heart tug, and I identified with that sinful woman! I was feeling that I had *much* for which I needed forgiveness!

The lesson Jesus was teaching in that passage was that a person who has been forgiven more will love Him more, and a person who has been forgiven little will love little.

That lesson was very *meaningful* and *encouraging* to me! I knew that I wanted it to be true in my life, that if Jesus could forgive me of so much, that I would love him more!

I felt sure that God had led me there to the church building that Sunday morning just to hear that!

TWELVE

Moving Forward with More Disappointment

Life went on and gradually became a little more normal as I continued with my teaching career and my involvement with my boys and their activities.

After a few years, I met someone who was to become my third husband. Not wanting to jump into anything again, as I had done before, we went together for two and a half years before getting married.

When I met my third husband, I felt like we had much in common. Both of us had grown children, and we both were in education professions. Until we got married, we taught in different counties. He was a breath of fresh air to me! He was attractive, he had a good personality, and we had fun together.

This became a time in my life when I felt like I could now focus more on some things that I wanted to do. Since all the boys had graduated from high school and were moving on with their lives, I no longer felt like I was needed at home as much. If I wanted to, I could now go out and have fun doing different things with different people in different places.

At first, my third husband and I lived and worked in different towns, about two and a half hours apart. That left the weekends for us to see each other, and many of those weekends we spent together. I thought I had actually finally found some happiness for myself, and after all I had been through, I told myself that it was about time! I deserved it! I was ready to have some fun and enjoy life again!

With the boys having graduated from high school, and with little help on the farm, I began to feel the enormity of the responsibility of taking care of everything on the farm by myself. I had stayed there after my first two divorces, until the boys had all graduated from high school, and for a time, the boys and others had provided help along the way. Now that I was by myself most of the time, the farm was beginning to become too much for me to think about or to care for on my own.

It was hard to think about selling the home place as we all had so many good memories there. But living there alone, I knew I could not take care of a seventy-six-acre farm by myself forever. With all the considerations at the time, I had a *hard choice* to make.

I finally decided that I needed to sell the house and some of the acreage, which I did! Then I began to sell different plots of land, and eventually, I sold the remaining lots in my ABC Estates subdivision that I had developed after my first divorce. I also gave each of the boys some acreage from the farm for them to use as they saw fit.

In the back of my mind was the thought that I might someday want to move. After going with someone for a few years, our relationship had progressed to the point where I was again considering remarriage. I was thinking that, if the relationship continued to progress, I could possibly begin a new life in a new town, which no doubt would mean lots of changes. Among those would be a different job, new extended family members, new friends, a new house, and a new church.

In 1990, after getting a teaching position in a town near where my future third husband was living, I resigned my first-grade position from H. W. Wilkey Elementary School where I had taught since the school had been built and first opened. I had enjoyed so many good years there, and I knew I would miss all the friends I would be leaving behind.

I had been fortunate to work *with* and learn *from* so many good teachers in that school, which included all my fellow first-grade teachers. Over the years there, I also spent a lot of good times with other teachers as well. Even today, I still have contact with several of those Wilkey teachers who I still consider as good friends.

While teaching at H. W. Wilkey Elementary School, I had many wonderful first-grade students and parents who made my years there so enjoyable. It is always especially rewarding to hear of the success of one of my former students, to run into one of them or one of their parents and hear a story of them as a successful adult, or to learn that they now have children or grandchildren of their own.

After leaving my teaching position at H. W. Wilkey Elementary School in Leitchfield, Kentucky, and after marrying for the *third* time and moving to Monticello, Kentucky, I was again teaching first grade, only at a different school. I remained as a first-grade teacher at Walker Elementary School in Wayne County for four years, and for the next four years, I was the elementary principal there.

The first years while living in Monticello with my third husband were good years. I enjoyed going to many basketball games with him, as he was one of the basketball coaches when we got married. Most every weekend, when he didn't have a basketball game, we would leave town and go to Lexington. He had lived in Lexington in previous years, and he knew lots of people whom we would see and socialize with on weekends when we were there.

In the earliest years of our marriage, we worked in our respective schools all week and then were off to Lexington for the weekend to have fun. This was our usual pattern. Life was good again! But, as is often true in a relationship when the newness wears off, there were soon to be some bumps in the road ahead.

One of those occasions was when my daddy died. That was a very hard time for me! The last time I saw Daddy was in 1993, when he was at my house in Monticello to celebrate his May 6 birthday. We had jointly celebrated his birthday and Mother's Day with Mama, as Mother's Day was coming a little later in the month. To make it personally more difficult for me, Daddy died near the end of the school year, which was a busy time for me as a teacher. During that time of grieving, I felt far away from my family members, who I knew all shared my personal grief but were not close by for support. Thankfully, a fellow teacher (God rest her soul) stepped up to help me with my teaching duties by finishing my record book and end-of-year reports for that year. We both taught first grade right across the hall from each other, and I so very much appreciated her help. We became good friends, and we remained so, even after retirement and up until her death a few years ago.

A few years after we married, my husband quit coaching and became the assistant high school principal. From that time on, our lives seemed to change. I was the head principal at Walker Elementary School at the time, and we both had individual responsibilities at our own schools, which brought a lot of necessary changes to our lives. I found myself working long and hard hours as I wanted to be successful and took my new responsibilities very seriously. At the same time, I was basically taking care of most of the responsibilities of running our household.

There were many times when I felt compelled to take care of a job or home responsibility that made it harder to always accompany my husband as I might have done in the previous years. It caused a lot of conflict when we did not agree on what I felt I needed to do with my position as principal and what he thought I should do.

I did not feel I could just pick up and go every time he might want me to leave, whether it was to go to Lexington, to his mother's house, or to one of *his* school activities. To take care of my job responsibilities, I often was needed at my *own* school, sometimes on weekends, and often at odd hours. As the head principal, I was ultimately responsible for anything that happened at my school. I felt I needed his support with my job, and it caused a lot of conflict when we did not agree on *my* job responsibilities.

Many times, he would just leave if we had disagreements. He might go to Lexington for the weekend without me, or he'd go to his mother and dad's house in a nearby town to stay, sometimes for a few days at a time. I was actually very fond of his parents, and I had always tried to accompany him whenever I felt I could work it in with my own job and family responsibilities, but it was harder for me to go with him to visit them as often as I had before I became a principal.

Both my father and my husband's father had died within a few years after we married. My mother was now living by herself after Daddy died, and I had hoped to try to visit with her more often as I could find time. His mother lived closer to us than my mother, so it was easier and less time-restrictive to go there for a visit. It took more of an effort to visit my mother, but visiting with her was important to me.

Although he would occasionally go with me, I felt I received very little support, as on most of my visits, I ended up going alone. As a compromise, I suggested that we alternately choose weekend activities or visitations, but that did not prove to be a satisfactory solution.

Another conflict arose when my grandchildren were born. Several of them were born within a few years, from two different sons. Before I had any grandchildren, I had welcomed his children and grandchildren into our home and had enjoyed having them there and had helped care for them. I liked his family! When my grandchildren were born, I wanted him to try to understand how important they were to me, and that I wanted to see them and spend time with them as well. Grandchildren became an important focus for me, and I had hoped both his and mine would be important focuses for us both.

We had many areas of disagreement, which included these family priorities as well as job responsibilities. Other differences and disagreements were in the areas of money, finances, and how we spent our weekends.

I wanted us to go to church together on Sundays, and we *did* on a few occasions, but not on a regular basis. Being gone out of town so much on weekends was not very conducive to that. I realize I could have gone by myself, but I didn't. That's on me!

My excuse was that I didn't want the controversy, so I got out of the "habit" of attending a church service on Sunday. I tried not to think too much about missing church to do something else that was fun, but deep down, I usually felt guilty. It was like I was putting God and church on the back burner.

For many months, when we tried to have a conversation about our differences, we could never seem to reach a consensus, and nothing ever changed.

In retrospect, I feel one mistake we made before we got married was not discussing in more depth and detail the blending of our families and how we might have become "set in our own ways" after being on our own for quite a while. Blending families can often be very difficult under the best of circumstances, but one would think that two reasonably intelligent people with our backgrounds would be able to reach a mutually satisfactory agreement. However, that did not prove to be the case for us.

I thought I would spend the rest of my life with my third husband. I enjoyed being with him, and we usually had a good time together. I liked his family—all his children, his grandchildren, and his parents. But for so long, after not being able to work through our differences, it seemed as if our marriage had somehow become a competition, rather than a cooperative effort where we *both* were willing to make compromises and have heartfelt discussions of our different ideas, feelings, and thoughts. In addition, as I look back, I now believe there was some unresolved emotional baggage from previous relationships that we should have discussed and resolved before getting married.

After many months, with little progress in settling our differences, my disappointment with my present situation really began to come into focus one Sunday afternoon. Having spent another one of our weekends in Lexington, we were driving back to Monticello.

On the way back, I was listening to a tape of Roy Clark songs. A song written by Kris Kristofferson started playing that caught my attention. Some of the words were very meaningful to me. I was *convicted* by some of the words I was listening to from the song, "Why Me." The entire song was compelling, but especially the following lyrics:

> … Lord help me Jesus, I've wasted it so
> Help me Jesus I know what I am.
>
> Tell me Lord, if You think there's a way
> I can try to repay
> All I've taken from You
> Maybe Lord, I can show someone else
> What I've been through myself
> On my way back to You.

That song kept speaking to me! For days, and even weeks, I played that song *over* and *over*!

I was beginning to feel like I had wasted a lot of years just *having fun*. Not that having fun is bad! Having fun can be a good thing, but I was beginning to realize that I did not have my priorities straight! I knew that someway, somehow, I needed to get back to where I needed to be in my walk with God. Deep down, I knew I was not putting God first!

My dissatisfaction grew without any of our differences being settled. Obviously, my husband's dissatisfaction grew as well, as he had divorce papers delivered to me one day by the county sheriff at my school office. Even after that unexpected happening, we continued living together for quite some time afterward.

Friends came through for me again during these troubled times, and I was especially blessed by the support of several. My secretary and her husband supported me in various ways. My superintendent and his wife became good friends who supported me in every way, even to the point that they traveled many miles to the funeral home when my daddy, and later my mother, died. I appreciated them all, and I continue to value their love and friendship to this day.

Suddenly, a new door opened! With the passing of a new Kentucky law, I learned I could receive full retirement benefits if I was fifty-five and had at least twenty-seven years of service credit. At the end of the school year, I would have thirty years of credit, and I was fifty-five, so *with a divorce hanging over my head*, I decided I was going to retire at the end of the school year when I had finished all my administrative duties at the end of June. I gave my notice, made all the plans, and retired at the end of the school year in 1998.

I enjoyed my years living in Monticello and have been back on a few occasions. Even with a few disappointments, I met a lot of good people while living there, and I think fondly of many of them and remember the many kindnesses shown to me as we interacted throughout the years. My original reason for moving there was to be with my third husband who had now filed for a divorce, so under the circumstances, I didn't see much of a future for me there. Our lives had been back and forth for too long, and I so much wanted and needed a more peaceful life.

The year I retired, I bought a house in Lexington, Kentucky, and I thought I would be moving there by myself. My husband already owned a house in Lexington. When he unexpectedly also decided to retire that same year, I held out some hope for reconciliation. Even though he had filed for divorce, he had done very little to follow through with it, so we decided to try again together in Lexington. Sadly, it wasn't long before the same old arguments and destructive behaviors followed, with still no resolution!

We had tried counseling several times, with different counselors while still in Monticello, but with no success. We had settled none of our differences, and at this point, if we were to work things out, I was convinced that we would have to make some concessions with each other and learn to communicate our feelings in an honest way, either by ourselves, through church, or through another counselor. So we agreed to begin counseling again for the *fifth* time in Lexington.

We went to counseling a few times together and then had individual meetings with the counselor separately. After a few meetings, I was the only one who continued to see him or to follow any of his suggestions.

I wanted to try to save my marriage, so I continued with the counselor for over a year by myself. My counselor didn't promise that he could save my marriage, but he did say that, if I stayed with him long enough, he could help me. And he *did*!

During this time, it became increasingly evident to me that there was no longer a *mutual commitment* to save our marriage, and by now, the divorce had been hanging over my head for over five years. I knew it was impossible for me to have a relationship by myself!

At that point in my life, I felt I had been successful in many ways, except for the thing I had wanted most: having a happy marriage! I had failed for the third time!

I had another hard decision to make and could see no good choices! So, once again, I just had to run over the skunk!

T H I R T E E N

Getting out of a Rut

At this time in my life, I was living in Lexington and was alone again. All my immediate family members lived in other Kentucky towns almost two hours away.

By now, six of my seven grandchildren had been born (Addison, Bradley, Landon, Alana, Brooklyn, and Allison) and the seventh (Elijah) was on the way. I had hoped to see them more often and to spend quality time with them, and to see my sons and daughters-in-law more frequently after I retired. I knew I could now see them much more if I were going to be by myself, or if my marriage was over.

I had spent my life loving and enjoying children, I had dearly loved having my own sons with me for their growing-up years, and now I could enjoy having that experience with my own grandchildren. In addition, I would be able to spend more time with my mother, who had now been a widow for several years.

Knowing what I had been going through since retiring and moving to Lexington, my daughter-in-law sent me a note one day that said Barry (my middle son) had requested prayers for me at church, that he wanted me to find true happiness, and that he loved me very much and was worried about me. The following (I kept a copy) is my response, which was an indication of how I was feeling at that particular time:

Dear Barry, Gail, Bradley, and Allison,

I was very touched when you wrote me that you all were praying for me, and that Barry had requested a prayer for me for my true happiness. I guess I cried for about five minutes. I often wonder how I could have such great kids when I feel like sometimes I have let them down by not being able to have them see an example of what I believe to be the kind of marriage and family that God intended. I realize I did not have control over the entire situation, but I sometimes feel that I have been such a failure in that area of my life.

I'm really trying to work through some of those feelings of failure and inadequacy, especially now that I'm getting older and have time to think and ponder since I've retired. I really am *not* miserable, but I guess the best way I can explain it is that I am having a lot of painful thoughts, while I am trying to look back at my life and trying to understand why some of the things have happened to me and why I made some of the choices I did. In another respect, I am working on trying to become more and more at peace with myself as I try to work on my personal relationship with God.

I guess I thought I was supposed to be perfect, and I didn't want anyone to see any faults I might have had, especially not my parents or children. And maybe I thought that if I just did enough, I would have a husband who would love me for it. I think that God intended for married love to be a gift to each other, not because either is good enough or perfect enough, but because of their unconditional love for each other.

I also believe it is true that we can never do enough or be good enough to earn our salvation. That is a gift that comes to us by the grace of God.

I think it is probably true that it is much easier for God to forgive us when we "goof up" or make bad choices, than it is for us to forgive ourselves for our mistakes, or for others to forgive us. That is a big part of what I'm trying to come to terms with now.

I really and truly feel my life is now going in the right direction, even though I'm not quite sure exactly where that is in some respects, but I believe God will let me know. Don't worry about me. Just keep praying for me, as I do for you all. I love you very much. Give Brad and Allison a hug for me; they are so, so, so precious—more important than anything else you'll ever have.

Love,
Mom

I was beginning to make some changes, but I felt like I was still stuck in a rut! It was easier to just keep plodding along, to stay on the same path and stay in the rut instead of making the effort to get out. I may have gotten too comfortable there. I logically knew I couldn't just keep on doing the same things in the same way over and over and expect to get different results.

I knew that the statute of limitations for blaming others for my perceived problems and unhappiness had run out for me! *No one but me* was responsible for my behaviors and choices. And now, only by looking *within my own self,* could I successfully grow and change.

> People are just about as happy as they make up their minds to be.
> —Abraham Lincoln

At first, I felt I had the tools and skills at my disposal to get out of the rut by myself. After all, I was relatively intelligent. I could take care of myself. I was strong enough. But I began to gradually realize just how deep the rut was, and how weak I really was. I needed something or someone else to help me get out. So I began *searching*, and I continued to search for quite some time.

> If you don't like something, change it, if you can't
> change it, change the way you think about it.
> —Mary Engelbreit

I had been listening for too long to music that made me feel sorry for myself, that made me feel like I had been mistreated, rather than listening

87

to songs that were inspiring and uplifting. I was basically "crying in my beer," feeling like a martyr, singing a somebody-done-me-wrong song, and hearing from others that it wasn't fair what had happened to me! I had always liked country music, and I still like a lot of it, but I decided to start listening to more gospel music or happy songs, and before long, I realized I had become a big fan of gospel quartets and the Gaither Vocal Band, which was far more uplifting.

> Change your thoughts and you change your world.
> —Norman Vincent Peale

I bought many, many self-help books, and I read many, many articles as I was trying to find out what was missing in my life and how to fix it. I had several single friends who were kind enough to share their time with me, to invite me to various activities, or to provide moral support. Friends helped tremendously, but there was still something missing.

I tried to form new relationships with a few other men, and I even continued to go out with my third ex-husband on occasion, as I had always enjoyed his company and had a good time with him. But something was still missing. I did not have that happiness and contentment I so desperately craved. I was *happy* at times, but there was no lasting *peace* and *contentment* in my life.

> You don't drown by falling in the water, you drown by staying there.
> —Edwin Louis Cole

One Saturday night, I had gone out to a pub with friends, and somehow, I began talking to a stranger. During the course of our conversation, the subject of religion came up. I discovered he was also a BUICK (Brought-Up-In-Church Kid). We found we had something in common, as we both had experienced failed relationships. We had also both grown up going to church on a regular basis but had gotten out of the habit of going regularly.

I had tried several different local churches, but after a few Sundays at each, I did not go back. I had not as yet found a home church in Lexington. So this stranger and I decided we would meet the next day and attend church together, and we did!

We decided to meet at Southland Christian Church, which was a large church close to where I lived. I had been there a few times and liked the fact that it was a big church. At that particular time in my life, I just wanted to get lost in the crowd. I didn't care if anyone knew my name, and I didn't want people asking me any questions. So, the next day at the Sunday morning service, I met the person I had talked to the night before, and we sat through the service together.

On that particular Sunday, the minister's lesson grabbed my attention, and it turned out to be very meaningful. It was a *turning point* for me where I began to find *greater* healing. The lesson was entitled, "Jesus: A Friend of the Brokenhearted." My own heart had been broken several times, and he was talking to me—or, as I truly believe, Jesus was speaking to me through him. He quoted Sue Monk Kidd, who said, "It's sad to come to the place in your life where you know all the words, but none of the music." I felt that so accurately described my life!

I cried through most of that sermon. I felt convicted! I realized that was the Holy Spirit at work in my heart. I knew I had not been living according to what my own conscience told me was right and wrong, and for several weeks afterward, I did a lot more crying, both alone and at other church services.

I do not know the name of the stranger I had met the night before who attended church with me that Sunday morning, and I never saw him again, but I later thought he was perhaps an *angel* sent from God.

While continuing to attend church at Southland, I was also encouraged by another minister who sometimes presented the lesson. In one very unforgettable lesson, he spoke words which caused me to really question my own salvation: "You can't really be happy until you are ready to die!"

For many years, I had not been truly happy, so I thought I must not be ready to die!

I had experienced many moments of happiness, many ups and downs, many victories and defeats. Many times, I had been on top of the mountain, and at other times, I had been down deep in the valley, but there was always in the back of my mind something that was missing.

On the outside, it might have seemed to some that I had it all together, but I sometimes felt like I was dying inside! I was tired of all the turmoil, struggle, and strife. I just wanted to feel rested and at peace.

I knew deep down that I had made a lot of mistakes and sometimes felt so unworthy, so inadequate and guilty. I could not be as perfect as I wanted to be, or as others expected me to be. I did a lot of pretending, and I may have fooled a lot of people, but little did they know the times I cried alone and felt like a phony. I knew I needed to get real—and get back to God!

It was about that time when I recalled some words from the song "Why Me" that I had played so many times, and which I had never forgotten. "Maybe Lord, I can show someone else what I've been through myself on my way back to You." My sincere hope was that I could *somehow, some way get back to God*, and maybe in some way—by word or by example—help others to do the same!

Self-help books, family, friends, and counselors all had been of help to me. But it was finally clear to me that really *surrendering my life to God* had been the missing ingredient. I realized that, at painful times in my life, I had been in a struggle to be in total submission to God's will for my life, and that caused a lot of my misery, unhappiness, and inner turmoil.

I had wasted a lot of months, and even years, thinking I was strong enough and smart enough to help myself get out of my rut on my own. It wasn't until I was too tired to go any farther on my own, that I let go of some of my foolish pride and was now trying harder to surrender my will to God's will for my life. That was surprisingly such a relief! I felt like I had been *set free*, and now I had a renewed strength to go on and continue to heal!

I remembered something I had once read or heard that (paraphrased) certainly described how I was then feeling: "When a person gets to his wit's end, he'll find that God lives there."

I continued attending Southland Church for several years and was always encouraged by the lead minister, who was an excellent teacher. I had found Southland Christian Church to be a welcoming and nonjudgmental place where I was allowed to heal. I later became a member at Southland and continued going there until I moved and left Lexington. My time there was an important part of my healing and my growth as a Christian.

Healing had been a gradual process for me, and in many ways, it is still ongoing. I felt like I was sometimes taking two steps forward and one step backward. I had spent most of my life praying for *what I wanted from God and what I wanted Him to do for me* without ever really asking God *what He wanted from me and what He wanted me to do for Him.*

I was now starting on a more peaceful journey. I knew that, in addition to the many pleasures of life that hopefully would lay ahead, there would still be bumps, hills, and valleys. However, I felt sure that I would now be on a smoother and more peaceful journey as I started in a new direction. I had experienced forgiveness, and I recognized that I had an internal GPS (the Holy Spirit) to help guide me as I continued on with my journey. The journey was becoming more beautiful! I was again enjoying the trip, with so many beautiful sights along the way. I became more confident that I was now moving toward my final destination of Heaven. My newly increased awareness of my forgiveness and assurance of my salvation helped me to begin to find an inner peace that I had never known before.

My thinking was continuing to change and to be refined.

Perhaps God *had* answered my prayers after all!

Maybe He said no! Maybe it wasn't His will for me to have a happy marriage for which I had always prayed.

Maybe I didn't need to be married to be happy.

Maybe He wanted me to serve Him as a single, thrice-divorced person.

Maybe God hadn't actually "joined me together" with the men I had married.

Maybe God had a different purpose for my life.

What was it that God really wanted for my life?

What is happiness? Is it the same as contentment, peace, and joy?

What are my God-given spiritual gifts, and how can I use them to help others?

I didn't have all the answers, but I was very confident that I was *now* beginning to ask some of the important questions, and that day by day, God was revealing new truths to me.

> If God answers your prayers, He is increasing your faith.
> If He delays, he is increasing your patience.
> If He does not answer ... He has something better for you.
> —Sharifah Nor

FOURTEEN

New Endeavors in a New Town

I certainly did not have all the answers, but I now felt I was at least heading in the right direction. I knew I had a long way to go, and I might never completely get there, but I was at least getting better. I found myself looking for new interests and challenges.

For the next several years after my third divorce, I began to focus on what I determined should be my priorities in life, what I called the five Fs: *faith, family, friends, finances, and fun*—and in that order!

I could now pursue my own interests. I could go where I wanted to go. I could do what I wanted to do with family and friends. I didn't have to answer to anyone in a relationship. I began to enjoy my independence, after years of trying to please someone else without seemingly much success. I was beginning to like myself again, and I didn't have to worry about not being accepted by someone just because I might have put on a few extra pounds or added a few more wrinkles.

I had a group of single friends with whom I enjoyed spending time in various ways. I enjoyed diverse activities with several friends, all of whom were especially kind to me. I appreciated them all and valued their friendship, as they helped me to begin to move on with my life. As time passed and we all experienced life changes and our extended families grew, some of our priorities changed, and some of the friends developed other interests. I found I especially had many common interests with three of these friends, and we began to spend a lot of time together. I still consider these ladies very special after all these years, and even after moving to a different city, we still keep in touch.

I shared fun and interesting outings, trips, and vacations with some of my Lexington friends. Some of us went to Boston to the AARP convention one year, where we also toured and saw many of the historical sites. Another year was a trip to the AARP convention in Chicago. We took road trips or bus trips to nearby states. We went to plays and concerts. Some of us would often get together to watch a NASCAR race or a Kentucky basketball game. We met at different times for holidays or birthday celebrations. Whatever we did, and wherever we went, it usually included good food and drink and was always a good time.

I enjoyed being with and talking to like-minded people who shared a common interest, so I decided to join the Republican Women's Club, and I met so many nice ladies at our monthly meetings. It was refreshing to be around ladies who obviously loved our country, when much of what I heard on the daily news was so very negative and often seemed so un-American. There were many women in our club who devoted much time, energy, and effort to working for the betterment of our community, state, and country. Some of them spent much more time on worthwhile activities than I did, and I considered them true patriots.

For a few years, one of my roles in the club was as our Americanism chairman, and later, I became the state Americanism chairman. I enjoyed that position as I did research and made presentations on historical and political events that I shared at different meetings. I learned a lot while doing all this research. With each new nugget of information, I gained even more appreciation for many of the great contributions of men and women of the past, or other significant details of the history of our state, nation, or community.

Working with a fellow member made it possible to compile and document several of the historical or America-related articles which I had presented. With her help, the articles were then archived and made available for use by other clubs around the state.

Another rewarding activity for me was as an election poll worker in my precinct. This meant going to training and then working long, hard hours on election days, but it was very satisfying to me to think I might be making a small contribution as a good citizen.

A few years after moving to Lexington, I had enrolled in the H&R Block tax course as I wanted to learn how to do my own taxes, instead of paying someone else to file them. After I finished the course, I was offered a job and ended up working for the company for fourteen years doing seasonal work.

For a while, I wondered if my first-day work experiences might be a jinx, as my first day of tax training was on September 11, 2001, and my first day of teaching had been on the day when President Kennedy was assassinated. Ultimately, both professions turned out to be rewarding and enjoyable for me, even though for our country—*and* for me—they were both very memorable days.

Working for H&R Block as a seasonal employee was a good fit for me. I had retired from being an elementary principal, and I really didn't want a full-time, year-round job anymore. I wanted to be able to spend time with my grandchildren and other family members. That was one of the main reasons for taking my retirement at an early age.

I liked the tax office where I worked. My coworkers and I became friends who got along and worked well together, helping each other and learning from each other. I enjoyed the challenge of trying to find answers to tax questions and in seeing and becoming friends with my clients. I always looked forward to seeing my clients again the following tax year.

After continuing my employment as a seasonal employee for fourteen years with H&R Block, I ended my years there as a senior tax advisor. There were many excellent opportunities for me to learn more about taxes, finances, and business by taking advantage of all the continuing education courses offered each year.

Over the years, I continued to expand my knowledge about tax preparation and related areas, which proved to be a significant help to me with my personal finances. Since I resigned from my position as a tax advisor, inasmuch as possible, I have continued to use some of that information to help friends and family members.

For several years after my third divorce, I would occasionally run into my third ex-husband, and we might even plan to do something together. We were cordial to each other, but we had basically gone our own ways. We continued to have somewhat of a connection for many years, as I continued to file his taxes for him as long as I continued to work at the tax office. Since I left my position at the tax office, I have not seen him, and I have had no contact at all with him since I moved to Bowling Green. Time spent with him was an important part of my life and growth experiences, and I truly hope he has found happiness and peace for himself.

During this particular period of my life, I had been going to church on a regular basis and usually went in alone and often sat alone. I sometimes would become a little teary-eyed when I saw an older couple sitting in front of me, holding hands, or with the man having his arm around the lady's shoulder, or when he would help her with her coat. I had always so much admired what I called old-fashioned manners as to how a man might treat a lady. For a few minutes, I would be saddened by thinking what *might have been* or *could have been*, and how nice it would be to grow old with someone I loved doing those things for me. I wished that I could have what they seemed to have. But I didn't!

It seemed that most of the men I met at that stage in my life seemed to want what I referred to as a "nurse with a purse". They seemed to want someone to take care of them, and then a woman who could afford to financially take care of herself. I knew there would have to be some strong mutual feelings and major considerations discussed before I ever decided to commit to another serious and permanent relationship.

Shortly thereafter, I met a nice man with whom I developed a friendship. He came to church with me and actually *did* have old-fashioned manners and *did* do all the little things that I admired. He treated me special and was good to me in so many ways. As the days passed, it became obvious that he wanted a more serious and permanent relationship than I did. He had many admirable qualities which I liked and appreciated, but there were too many important areas in which we did not agree. While I liked him very much, I did not want to make the commitment that might lead to marriage.

Thankfully, after many years of mistakes, I felt I had better learned to communicate my feelings than I had done in previous relationships, and I knew I needed to be honest with him. I was happy with the way my life was progressing, and I did *not* want an exclusive, intimate relationship. That proved to be a deal-breaker, and shortly thereafter, we cordially ended the relationship. Within a year after we parted ways, I learned that he had married. I was very happy to hear that he had found happiness with someone else.

During these years, my extended family grew and changed. Each year, we had an annual family reunion, with each of us six siblings rotating as host or hostess every six years. We began the reunions annually after Daddy died, and each year, there was something new or different to report.

There were always celebrations, as well as regrets and sad news to share when we got together. From year to year, there might have been high school and college graduations, weddings, divorces, family struggles, children born, and grandchildren born. It was always good to know that whatever was going on in a family member's life, there would always be other family members to provide support and encouragement.

One of our favorite places to get together was at my brother and sister-in-law's farm—the home place in Big Clifty, Kentucky, where we all grew up. Another wonderful venue was Five Star Retreat in Nunnelly, Tennessee, which was owned by my nephew who, for many years, generously allowed us all to meet there and use his wonderful lodge, cabins, and other retreat facilities at his own expense. There were always so many fun things for all ages to do at those two beautiful locations. Wherever we met, even when at various other locations, our annual family reunion was always a *good time for all!*

One of the things I enjoyed over these years at the reunions was trying to add humor to some of our reunions, especially when it was my turn to be the hostess. I have always enjoyed humor, specifically, the innocent humor of children, humorous movies, books, sayings, and many fun times with my sisters who can all be crazy funny at times.

My siblings and I rotated years to be the host or hostess at our reunions. One year when it was my year to be the hostess, I dressed up in a long, blond wig and told "dumb blond" jokes. That year is especially memorable to me as my oldest grandson was just a few years old. Addison was normally very loving to me, but when he saw me that day, he was afraid of me. He would have nothing at all to do with me, as long as I had on that silly blond wig.

One of my hostess years, I dressed up as an old grandma. I was the old, "Grey-Haired-Granny" who gave advice to everyone in the younger generation. I'm not sure if it was actually good advice, or if any of them remembered it, but I had a lot of fun dishing it out!

Another year when it was my turn to be hostess, *Duck Dynasty* was the craze. We had a *Duck Dynasty* theme with various activities revolving around that theme. Two of the *Duck Dynasty* characters, Willie and Uncle

Si, "made an appearance" at the reunion. I enlisted the help of two of my sons, Alan and Barry, to play the characters and share some of the Robertson's family humor that I had compiled.

I think all the parents of the younger kids got mad at me that year as I had given everyone there a duck whistle to blow. Each person was supposed to blow their whistle anytime they were having fun or saw something they liked. I think most of the grown-ups got tired of hearing all the younger kids blowing those whistles all day, but occasionally, they would be the ones guilty of blowing the whistle themselves.

Another humorous activity I have enjoyed over the years was finding materials, preparing materials, personalizing the materials, and then using the materials to give birthday roasts for family members and friends when they were celebrating a special birthday, such as a seventieth, seventy-fifth, or eightieth.

My sense of humor may be viewed by some as acting silly. I think that may be somewhat of a carryover from teaching and being around young children for so many years. I love young kids! Young kids are fun! To me, just watching and listening to them is entertaining! Young kids respond to silliness! Actually, humor and laughter are good medicine for adults, too, and most of us as adults could use a little more laughter in our lives! Sometimes, it might be good for us to let go, or chill and have fun, like the little kids!

Since moving to Lexington, my life had become very different. Nothing stays the same! I had gone through many changes since I had moved there. There were some difficult times, when I might have been sad for days. Then there were the happy times which I always hoped would never end. I knew more than likely in the years ahead, there would be more good times as well as bad times. However, I was now more confident that, in the future, I would be better at dealing with either or both!

FIFTEEN

Grandchildren—Seven Is My Lucky Number

It had been a gradual process over a period of about ten years, but I was enjoying life again. I was healing and getting closer to God. I was becoming more positive, more grateful, more joyful, and more thankful that God had always provided for my needs. I was thankful for His salvation and forgiveness, and for the family with whom I had been blessed. In this phase of my life, blessings of family—and, in particular, my *seven* grandchildren—were bringing much joy to me in so many ways.

By the grace of God, I had lived long enough to finally overcome many difficulties. I had become wiser after experiencing many personal failures, realizing many of my shortcomings, and seeking forgiveness. I knew I could not go back and do any of my life over. Life does not allow us to go back and fix what we have done wrong in the past, but it does allow for us to live each day better than our last one. Now with a renewed faith, I wanted to concentrate on being a better example and helping my kids and grandkids in whatever years I might have left.

I had not been a perfect parent. I knew my children would not be perfect parents. It would be important for us all to understand that grandkids would not be perfect, either. The most important thing we could do for them would be to shower them with love! So much love!

> Above all, love each other deeply, because love
> covers over a multitude of sins.
> —1 Peter 4:8, NIV

My grandchildren had become a major focus of my time and attention. I now had *seven* grandchildren: four grandsons and three granddaughters. I had always enjoyed the children I had taught in school, and now in my retirement, I found that my grandchildren were a wonderful source of love, enjoyment, and company.

I also found that I now had more time to spend with my three sons, their wives, and my aging mother as well. I knew how hard it was to be a parent. I was now older, and hopefully a little wiser. I wanted to try to help my children and their families in any way that I could and try to be a positive influence and a godly example to them all.

I was fortunate enough to enjoy many good vacation trips and other outings with my three sons and their families. I was frequently invited to go with them on their family vacations. I loved helping them out by being the in-house babysitter while we were on vacation, or keeping the grandkids at times when the parents might want to be gone alone. Keeping or watching the grandkids was never a chore. That was great enjoyment for me as I loved being around the grandkids, and if I could arrange it, I would go along or keep them any time I was asked.

I wish I could recapture every special memory of my seven grandchildren as they spent time with me in Lexington, or while on vacations or trips with them. Time spent with my grandchildren and their families were some of the best times of my life!

I tried to somewhat recapture a few of those memories of the special times I shared with my grandchildren in the memory book I made for each of them when they graduated from high school. Some of the important moments which were special to me were highlighted with pictures and comments from the time they were born until they graduated from high school.

The first grandchild is usually as exciting to a grandparent as the first child is to a parent. It is so amazing to watch a child begin to learn, and it's no wonder many grandparents brag that their grandchild is the smartest. It isn't until we have more grandchildren that we discover the unique and special qualities of each of them.

It was always so interesting and enjoyable for me to see the differences in each of my grandchildren. Just seeing those differences made me realize that God knew what He was doing when He made them. It is so astounding to see their different talents, personalities, and endearing charms.

> For you created my inmost being; you knit me together in my mother's womb. I praise you because I am fearfully and wonderfully made; your works are wonderful, I know that full well. My frame was not hidden from you when I was made in the secret place, when I was woven together in the depths of the earth. Your eyes saw my unformed body; all the days ordained for me were written in your book before one of them came to be.
> —Psalms 139:13–16, NIV

It took me a little while to get used to some of the differences between the boys and Alana, my first granddaughter. I had raised three sons, and my first three grandkids were boys, so she was different to deal with. She was so beautiful, sweet, dainty, and sensitive that I had to change some of my tactics with her, but as the first girl in the family for me, she was indeed very special.

Inasmuch as was possible when the grandchildren were with me, I tried to accommodate the wishes of the parents. After all, they were the ones who were now ultimately responsible for them. However, I'll have to admit, there was some spoiling! Isn't that what all grandparents do?

When Alan and Lou Ann's three children would come to visit me, it was their mother's wish that they all come together. That was fine with me. I had raised three together and could handle that. The first time I kept any of them was when I was living in Monticello before Alana was born. Alan and Lou Ann took a trip to California and left Addison and Landon with me. Addison was about three, and Landon was about eighteen months old at the time. Addison was obsessed with looking at my globe, spinning the globe, locating California, and putting his little finger on California to show me where his mama and daddy had gone. He also amazed me as a three-year-old by working a United States puzzle and correctly placing and identifying each state, and as he placed each state, he could also name all the state capitals.

When Addison, Landon, and Alana came to stay with me in Lexington, they usually had educational assignments to bring and complete. They were supposed to finish the assignment before we did the fun things I had planned, such as going to the GattiTown pizza buffet, to the game room, or to Bible miniature golf. My instructions were to have them finish their assignments before the spoiling began, and I always saw that they finished them first.

Even if they might not want to finish their assignments, they understood that educational assignments came first.

Landon was very intelligent and always made good grades, but he was the one who had always complained about hating school, and he might sometimes try to get out of finishing his assignment. One summer when they came, I remember Landon trying to use his charms on me, and in a pleading voice said, "Granny Pat, can we *please* just do something that is not educational?" He might have tried, but I think he always knew that assignments came first. Whether they liked it or not, the emphasis on education for all three of them paid off, as Addison, Landon, and Alana ended up getting academic scholarships to pay for their college educations.

I was fortunate to be able to enjoy many of the school activities in which Addison and Landon participated, most of which were academic team competitions. Alana was also a good student, but she seemed to be involved in more athletic endeavors than the boys, such as gymnastics and track meets. Several times, I enjoyed going to her gymnastic competitions and track events. The last one I remember attending was a track meet which was being run at the Kentucky Horse Park while I was living in Lexington.

I also had fun vacation times with Alan and Lou Ann's entire family. We went to Branson, Missouri, and the surrounding area together and enjoyed many shows, visited the Precious Moments Chapel, rode the duck boat on Table Rock Lake in the Ozarks, saw the *Great Passion Play*, and played miniature golf. We started a hole-in-one club, and any new or different place where we played miniature golf, everyone in the family wanted to be in that club. Sooner or later, we all *did* actually become members of that club.

We went together to Charleston one year, to Disney World, to Washington, DC, and to the Smoky Mountains. I think there might still be one of Landon's flip-flops somewhere at his parents' house, as he lost the other one in the creek on one of our multifamily Smoky Mountain trips. Something worse than losing a flip-flop could have happened if Landon's Uncle Cary had not jumped into the fast-moving waters of the Little

Pigeon River to save him as he was quickly being carried downstream in the swift waters.

My grandchildren, Bradley and Allison, were the children of Barry and Gail. Bradley was a very active child, and he seemed to want to try anything and everything, some of which often seemed overly adventurous to me. At home, for example, he made ramps and jumped his bicycle over them. I wasn't used to seeing that and was usually holding my breath while watching.

Allison was next to the youngest grandchild and was our little "miracle baby." She was a little preemie, weighing just a little over a pound when she was born. Barry could hold her in the palm of his hand. As a result, she always received a lot of pampering. She was so small for so long that a lot of Brad's friends would carry her around like a baby. This lasted until she was in middle school.

One year, Bradley and Allison were at my house while Barry and Gail had gone to the Kentucky Derby on the first Saturday in May. Bradley was big into skateboarding at the time and wanted to bring his skateboard. I made sure to get permission from his parents before he brought his skateboard, but that didn't prove to make any difference.

We went to the skate park, and as he was coming over a ramp, someone ran in front of him. He fell, and I noticed him holding his arm. He had a pitiful look on his little face, and with the way he was holding his arm, I could see it was broken. We went to the hospital, with me crying, saying I wished it were me instead of him. He was so brave! On the way to the emergency room, he was just calmly holding his little arm on the door rest while I continued to be upset. He could see how upset I was, and it turned out that he ended up being the one trying to comfort *me*, and telling *me* it would be all right.

Allison was a baby then, and I had to hold her all the time while we were at the hospital. She was so good while we were waiting. It was as if she could sense something was wrong, and that little sweet thing never made a peep the entire time we were there. We had to wait about two hours before a doctor could see Bradley and do X-rays. Even though he did have a broken bone, he had to wait from Saturday until Monday for the swelling to go down before getting a cast.

It was so hard for me to tell Barry and Gail after they came home from the Kentucky Derby that Bradley had a broken wrist. I felt like it was my fault. In all the time my three boys were growing up, I don't remember either of them ever having a broken bone, and now, years later, I had let Bradley get hurt.

I had Allison and Bradley in the bed with me with Bradley's little arm across the pillow when Barry and Gail came home. They were so sweet and understanding about it all. A few weeks later, on Mother's Day, they gave me a plaque thanking me for taking care of a little boy with a broken arm, as well as some other kind words. That made me feel a little better, but I still hated that it had happened on my watch.

Brad may have actually tried to get even with me later. I had gone to Bardstown one day to watch him play golf. I was walking along and watching as he played. I had walked ahead far on down the course from the tee. I stopped at a distance past where I thought he could possibly hit the ball. I was standing there, thinking I was out of range as he teed off. All of a sudden, *wham!* His golf ball hit me! I heard him yell, "I think I just killed my grandmother!" Thankfully, it had only hit my arm. It really hurt at the time, but by the time he finished his round, the sting was mostly gone, and we all laughed about it later.

Bradley liked staying at home more than some of the other grandkids, but one year he *did* come with a friend to stay with me for a week to attend a basketball camp in Lexington. He somehow became disillusioned with going to camp and decided he wanted to go home the day before it ended. He was very adamant about leaving, but Barry made him stay and finish the week. He stayed, but he was *not a happy camper.*

Allison often came to my house with Cary and Valerie's children, Brooklyn and Eli. Allison, Brooklyn, and Eli were the three youngest grandchildren, and by now, the older grandchildren were becoming involved in more activities of their own and could no longer find time to stay with me as often. Eli was born after I had retired and moved to Lexington, and this was after the older grandkids were more frequently pursuing their own individual interests.

Eli, Allison, and Brooklyn would often come together and stay with me. Although Allison often came with Brooklyn and Eli, there were times as they got older that I might go somewhere and take just *one* of the grandchildren, along with a friend of theirs. One particular solo event that

I especially enjoyed with Allison and one of her friends was on a trip to Nashville. We went to a boy band's concert one night and rocked the night away, having fun with the One Direction band. Several times, Allison, Brooklyn, or Eli would invite a friend, and I would enjoy just taking them on a fun trip or to celebrate some milestone accomplishment. We usually went to Pigeon Forge or Gatlinburg, Tennessee. I have many good memories of lots of those outings with grandchildren and their friends.

Even though all three of my boys and their families kept dogs in their houses, I had never kept a dog in my house. I liked dogs, but during these years, I didn't want to take care of one. I was gone from home too much.

One summer, when Brooklyn and Eli were coming for a visit, I drove to Elizabethtown to meet them. They had been with some other relatives and were now coming to stay with me for a few days before school started. After I was on my way back to Lexington, I discovered Brooklyn had not left the dog with the other relatives but had decided to sneak the dog to my house. She had it in her lap under a blanket. When I found out she had the dog, I think she was expecting me to be mad, but I didn't say anything. We just made the best of the situation and went to Walmart to get pads, food, treats, and toys for the dog, and we kept the dog and enjoyed playing with it until the kids went home.

Brooklyn was the grandchild who seemed to worry about me and always asked questions about me being alone and living by myself. On one visit when she was at my house, she told me that *we needed to go to Walmart.* When I asked her why she wanted to go, she said, "Granny Pat, you need a bird! I want to go buy you a bird so you will have someone to talk to!" Little did she know then what she probably knows now, that sometimes the quiet is nice!

When the younger three came to visit, and there wasn't any specific activity requested by the family, I sometimes made a schedule myself. I guess I still had a little of the teacher in me. I sometimes would make the schedule in advance and send it to them. They could get mail, and then they would bring the list with them when they came to visit. On the list I included chores to help me, things to do for others, as well as fun things. Each one coming was supposed to check their *first choice* of chores to do for me, something to do for others, and their *first choice* of fun things that they each wanted to do.

I wanted the grandkids to learn to think about others and not just always be thinking of themselves. So whoever was coming to visit could pick from the lists. They understood that the chores and things to do for others had to be done first. Then we would do their selected fun activity, such as going to the game room, going to the outdoor restaurant and feeding the ducks, playing miniature golf, or whatever else they might choose. I always made sure they each got to do their *own first choice* of the selected fun activity, but only after they finished their chores or good deeds.

One summer, the grandkids who had come for a visit decided they wanted to have a lemonade stand. They wanted to make money and share it! I thought, *Aha! A teaching moment, and some fun too!* I had good neighbors, and many of them stopped and bought lemonade when they saw the kids. All of us in the neighborhood did that for each other.

I had the grandkids write down everything they needed and the price of their lemonade stand supplies so they could figure their profit. After a few hours, when they sold out, they were excitingly counting their money. After they subtracted their expenses, I think they were a little disappointed, thinking they wouldn't get very much, as they figured they would have only a little over a dollar each and would have to give the rest to me for their expenses.

As you might guess, I ended up not charging them for the supplies, so they got to keep a little more. I probably couldn't let them have a lemonade stand today, as they would probably need to get a permit and would have to go by all kinds of rules, not to mention I might also get fined!

Even though I had plenty of room upstairs at my Lexington house, when the grandkids came to stay with me, they never wanted to sleep upstairs by themselves. I always put blankets and pillows on the floor in my downstairs bedroom, and no matter how many were there, they slept in the room with me. I didn't really care, as that way, I didn't have to worry about them getting up in the middle of the night and falling over the railing or down the stairs.

They would say that they were *afraid* of the *big pink pig* in the upstairs bedroom and didn't want to stay up there by themselves. That may have just been an excuse to stay downstairs with me, but it didn't matter! I wanted them to feel safe!

The *big pink pig* was a piggy bank that their grandfather and I had gotten many years before when we had gone to Mexico, and I had a lot of coins in it. Eli, my youngest grandchild, seemingly had more of a fascination with the pig than the others. He was always asking questions about it. Where did I get it? How much money is in it? Was I always going to keep it?

One day, amid all his questions, I told him that when I died, in my *will*, I was going to leave it to him. Then it would be his, and he could have all the money in it. That seemed to satisfy him! Sadly, a few years later, when I moved from Lexington to Bowling Green, the big pink pig somehow had gotten broken, and all the coins were all over the floor of the moving truck. After putting them all into a container to keep, I told Eli the next time I saw him that his pig had died! So he actually ended up getting all the coins early!

Barry and Cary's families loved going to the beach, and I enjoyed being able to go with them several times. I always had just as much fun as they did at the condo on the beach, whether at Panama City, Santa Rosa Beach, Gulf Shores, Destin, Clearwater, or Madeira Beach. I personally enjoyed the ocean views, sitting on the balcony, and the pools more than being in the actual sand. It was fun in the sand with the little kids, but just sitting by the pool or on the balcony looking at the ocean and listening to the sounds of the ocean was more relaxing for me.

When I was there on vacation with them, I helped out with the kids, or I did a lot of the cooking. I wasn't much of a shopper, so I usually stayed close to the condo or with the kids. We all enjoyed eating out at night and ate a lot of good, fresh seafood, and at other times, we ate fish the guys had caught while deep-sea fishing.

For several years, some of these family trips to the beach where I went along—with others of my family, as well as many of Valerie's family members—were in large part a result of the generosity of Cary and Valerie and the success of Cary's business at that time. I felt blessed and was always thankful and grateful to get to go along.

Charleston and Disney World were also good times spent with Barry and Cary's families. Several years, during the Thanksgiving holidays, many of our family members might be able to be at a large cabin in the Smoky Mountains for Thanksgiving dinner. Those who were there always pitched in to cook the Thanksgiving dinner. It was almost a given that one day, when we were in the Smoky Mountains, I would take all the kids and we would make a stop at the game room in Pigeon Forge and then on to Mel's Diner for ice cream or a milkshake.

Just think about it! There aren't very many places where you can have as much fun spending one hundred dollars as we usually did in the game room—and then only getting enough tickets to trade for a three-dollar prize! It may have been a waste of money to some, but it was worth it to me being with the kids and seeing them all having so much fun! And the truth was, I always had fun myself!

When I furnished the money, the rule was that everyone would equally share the tickets. It was always interesting to see which prizes the kids might pick, how they figured out what they could get, and how they bargained with each other when they might want to put their tickets together or save up for a bigger prize.

Game rooms were always a big hit with *all* my grandkids, young and old alike. The other game room we frequented a lot was at GattiTown in Lexington. There was also pizza to eat and movies playing there as well. I enjoyed many good times there over the years with *all seven* of my grandkids.

I liked meeting friends of my grandkids, and I enjoyed having them at my house. Several times, their friends would come along with my grandkids when we took little trips. We went to Pigeon Forge, Gatlinburg, and Florida on several occasions. We saw shows, toured various attractions, ate a lot, and of course, anywhere we went, we all tried to end up in a game room sometime during the trip. I liked being Granny Pat to all of them.

Many times, I was overwhelmed with such a sense of love and joy when I was around my grandkids. I might write something down just so I could remember it later. I'm sharing a couple of those memories exactly as I wrote them. The first one was written the day after a family wedding.

Sunday, 4/24/2005

Every once in a while, we have one of those "special unforgettable moments" which are such an awesome blessing. I had one of those last night.

It was at Randi and Nick's wedding reception. After the bride had shared the first dance with her new husband, and then the next dance with her father, the dance floor was open.

My youngest son, Cary, then took Brooklyn, his beautiful daughter, and my precious granddaughter, onto the dance floor. As he moved in his tuxedo, handsome at six feet four inches, and towering over her, they danced. Brooklyn, in her beautiful white dress with her upswept hair, looked like a princess! Cary occasionally bent down on Brooklyn's level to talk to her, and she would smile so sweetly at her daddy. Tears of love and happiness filled my eyes as I watched them together and thought of how, not so many years ago, Cary was just a little boy himself.

The beauty of the moment was even more wonderful as I watched my sweet, handsome little grandson, Eli, playing so innocently in his little tux in the background, oblivious to everyone and everything around him.

Shortly thereafter, I watched Cary as he danced with his beautiful wife, Valerie, my daughter-in-law, and I said a silent prayer for all of them. I prayed that they would always be together as a happy family, and that Cary and Valerie, as well as Brooklyn and Eli, would each find the peace of God that I had finally found after so many years. Oh, how I wish that I could protect them from all the hurt and heartache that undoubtedly they will face as the years pass.

The next entry was written when my three youngest grandchildren were at my house in Lexington for a visit.

7/14/2006
"Joys of Grandkids"

I am in a train station in my living room. I have a train station sign taped to my living room wall. There are phone numbers to call for tickets—for a station phone or a train phone. The ticket price is one dollar per mile. We have a scanner (a paddle) to scan, of course. The vacation train costs more.

There are little tickets, cut up with prices and stapled together, along with scissors and colored markers all over the living room.

There is an air mattress in my bedroom, with bags of clothes all around. Everyone brought their blankies too. Brooklyn, Eli, and Allison are staying while Cary and Valerie are gone to New York and New Jersey (Wednesday to Sunday).

I have entertained royalty! Brooklyn made crowns for everyone, and Allison and Brooklyn decorated them. They need their blankies for robes, and their scepters were part of the badminton poles, with dots and dips—dots for both "blessings" and "curses" to be pronounced on the subjects by the queen (Brooklyn), the princess (Allison), and the prince (Eli).

I'm drinking coffee while watching Eli eat his breakfast as he's sitting at the living room coffee table and watching cartoons. Brooklyn and Allison have gone upstairs to clean out the toy closet, one of their selected chores. We are all going to wash the car together later.

What fun to be a grandmother and watch the grandkids interact and play and pretend and learn. I always try to interject a little bit of wisdom as I can, trying to help develop kindness, tolerance, and consideration of others. The youngest three are here now, and I know times like these are precious—they'll soon be involved in their own "real" activities, as the older four grandchildren already are, to a large extent. I love having this time with them. I just hope they have some fond memories of Granny Pat when they are older.

A GRANDPARENT'S PRAYER

God, You have blessed me, indeed, as the child I love has had a child I love.

I *pray* that in Your mercy You watch over and protect my grandchildren as You have always done for me.

May their lives be long and healthy.

Fill them with Your grace, and bless them with every gift they need to live their lives in faithful obedience to You.

Touch their hearts and minds and fill them with wisdom, knowledge, hope, and understanding.

Help them to be loving, kind, and compassionate.

May they have the courage to follow You, and when the day comes when I am no longer on Earth with them, *may* they look back upon me with fond memories and *may* they never forget that they *were*, and *always will be*, deeply loved by me.

Lord, I place them in Your loving care and trust that You will always lead them, guide them, and love them.

Amen.

Partially adapted from Jane Craft and Catholic Christian

SIXTEEN

Later Years in Lexington

My seven grandchildren had basically grown up during the twenty years I lived in Lexington. I had been blessed to be able to spend a lot of time with them over the years while I was living there, watching them grow and mature.

I knew I could not go back and change anything I did or didn't do with my *own* children, but I had hoped that, by helping with my grandchildren, I could in some small way ease the responsibility of my own sons and their families in teaching and caring for *their* children. As a retired grandparent, I now had the *time* to spend with grandchildren, which at times had seemed so elusive to me when I was so busy with my *own* children.

As a parent, I often seemed to be part of the rat race with the busyness of raising a family, making a living, and dealing with my own problems. Now, years later as a grandparent, hopefully I have gained wisdom that I can share with the younger generations, my children and grandchildren.

Since retiring from a fulfilling career in education and moving to Lexington, I had developed new interests and had met new people, several of whom became good friends and with whom I enjoyed many happy times. For fourteen of these years, I had continued to work as a seasonal employee for H&R Block, which added a little extra financial help, as well as mentally challenging me to continue to learn.

It was during these years in Lexington that I discovered I could again have a beautiful, meaningful, and fulfilling life, even if things didn't turn out the way I had previously hoped or planned.

I had tried to accept responsibility for my own past behaviors and had sought and received forgiveness from others, inasmuch as was possible. Most importantly, I sought and received forgiveness from God. I was no longer blaming anyone else for my past failures, mistakes, and bad choices. I was looking forward to the future and trying not to live in the past. I more and more wanted to become a better person, a better example for my kids and grandkids.

I was continually trying to change my thinking, to focus more on the positive aspects of my life. I realized that, many times in the past, I had often asked God for help, but I often failed to say thank you when He answered. I was too focused on times when I thought He had *not* answered, and I had not accepted that He might be saying *no, not yet,* or *maybe later.* I became increasingly thankful and grateful for God's abundant blessings. I had begun to have a peaceful life, which I wanted to experience more and more. As I continued to become more positive and grateful, I found great encouragement in the following verses from Philippians 4:4–9 (NLT):

> Always be full of joy in the Lord, I say again- rejoice! Let everyone see that you are considerate in all you do. Remember the Lord is coming soon. Don't worry about anything, instead pray about everything. Tell God what you need, and thank him for all he has done. Then you will experience God's peace, which exceeds anything we can understand. His peace will guard your hearts and minds as you live in Christ Jesus. And now, dear brothers and sisters one final thing. Fix your thoughts on what is *true* and *honorable,* and *right,* and *pure,* and *lovely,* and *admirable.*
>
> Think about things that are *excellent_*and *worthy of praise.* Keep putting into practice all you learned and received from me-everything you heard from me and saw me doing. Then the God of peace will be with you.

Amid all the newfound peace and happiness I had *now* found, I knew there would be challenges to come, but I was also trusting that there would be periods of contentment and happiness as well. I was confident that, when they came, I could experience either of them, or both of them, from a different and renewed perspective.

Some of the happy periods that *did* come were in different years, while two of my grandsons were living with me. I was blessed to have my grandson Addison living with me one summer before he graduated from the University of Kentucky College of Engineering.

Addison was always so very pleasant to be around, and I also enjoyed meeting and entertaining several of his friends from Christian Student Fellowship at the University of Kentucky, where they were all members. I temporarily became their Granny Pat, and they all took advantage of my invitations to come over for meals several times. Later, when I saw those same boys on various other occasions, they still referred to me as Granny Pat, which would always bring a smile to my face.

It was also a blessing to have my grandson Landon living with me while he was finishing his engineering degree from the University of Kentucky. Landon and I were both big University of Kentucky fans and often enjoyed watching basketball games together. For a while, we had a pretty good partnership going as he would help me with computer, electrical, or mechanical concerns around the house, and I would in turn help him with his laundry or cook for him. His favorite meal was chicken tetrazzini, which he actually learned to make for himself while still living with me.

One of the challenges that came during these years, and which overall continued for a period of approximately eight years, was the declining health of my mother. She had lived by herself since my father had died in 1993. For several years, she managed fairly well. From the time Daddy died, she *did* have a lot of help and assistance from my younger brother and sister-in-law, who were always there for her during the first years when she was living alone. Both of them were wonderful to her! At that time, she was in relatively good health, and they lovingly helped her in so many ways. My older brother (God rest his soul), who was her doctor at the time, was also a big comfort and help to her when she had any medical concerns.

As Mama's memory declined, she needed to give up driving, which was a big change for her. She became more forgetful, she misplaced things, and she forgot to take her medicine, among other things. She just generally was beginning to need more help and support.

As parents get older, most of them prefer to continue living in their own homes, and that was true for Mama as well. For a while, my siblings and I tried to accommodate those wishes. We alternated days when we would call her, visit with her, check on her, or provide needed assistance so she could continue to live in her familiar surroundings. As the weeks passed, she began to feel more and more insecure by herself and began expressing the desire for one of us to stay longer or to be with her.

With the realization of Mama's needed assistance, one of my sisters and brother-in-law very graciously and lovingly took her to Nashville to live with them and to care for her, where she remained for approximately five years. Mama sold her house, took her favorite things with her, divided many of her belongings with all her children, and left the rest to be taken care of later. While living in Nashville with them, Mama was included in all their activities as much as was possible. They provided many wonderful opportunities for her to enjoy during the years she was with them. Many Nashville friends grew to love Mama, as she was included in Jane and Jesse's church, family, and social activities while she was living there.

During those years while Mama was living in Nashville, my other siblings and I would visit whenever we could, or we would provide love and support in some other significant way. Jane arranged to have help come in to give her a break, and whenever possible, one of my sisters or I would try to give Jane and Jesse some much-needed rest.

For a while, I continued to work at H&R Block and would often try to arrange days off so my sister Brenda and I could drive down to Nashville together to visit with Mama, which we tried to do at least every two weeks, and when possible, Mary Ann would fly in from California and stay several days to visit and help. My brothers would also help as well.

After a time, I began experiencing so much hip pain while going back and forth to visit with Mama—and while at work—that I decided to retire from H&R Block. I needed to focus more on my own health and on trying to provide support and help for Mama as much as possible.

Caring for Mama became increasingly challenging during those five years in Nashville. Jane was beginning to have some health concerns of her own, and my siblings and I began discussing other options, including a nursing home placement.

My siblings and I all knew Jane and Jesse needed a break, but to avoid a nursing home, at least for a little longer, it was decided that Mama would come to Lexington and live with me. She moved in with me in May of 2016. Whenever they could, my siblings all would then come to Lexington to visit with Mama.

Mama's memory got progressively worse during the months she was living with me. She still had times when her sense of humor was evident, and sometimes she could still converse with others, even if only in a limited way. As the months passed, she became more stubborn, uncooperative, angry, and sometimes very rebellious. She was becoming very different than the sweet Mama we all had known throughout our lives. We all understood, and sad as it was, we knew our mother was no longer her true, sweet self. She was suffering from the disease of Alzheimer's and had gotten progressively worse and worse.

All my own kids and grandkids got to spend some time with Mama in the last year of her life while she was living with me. They could all see how their Mamaw Duvall was declining, but a few times, even during the last few months, she might perk up for a few minutes and surprise us with her sense of humor or with something she would say.

My grandson Landon was living with me during the time Mama was there, and as soon as he would walk into the room, Mama's eyes would light up. He was a bright spot in her day, and he usually would sit down and talk to her for a few minutes. Even though she might not say a word, she would usually look at him lovingly and just smile.

Once, when my granddaughter Brooklyn had come for a visit, I was trying to get Mama to respond to her being there, and I was talking to Mama and said, "Mama, look! Your granddaughter Brooklyn is here to see you! Doesn't she look beautiful?" Mama looked at her for what seemed to be a long time, and then said, "Well, she doesn't look any better than I do!" It was moments like that when I could *smile* and remember my *real* mama!

I was fortunate to have two wonderful part-time caretakers who were such a help to me in caring for Mama. Many times, they could get her to do more than I could. They both had such patience with her, and the one who was there most often could usually get her to respond when I could not. During the time Mama was living with me, these two caretakers—along with my three sisters, Brenda, Jane, and Mary Ann, and my daughter-in-law Lou Ann—were also a source of wonderful personal help and support to me. They helped me in my recovery from two hip replacements. It was at times like those that I thanked God for the blessing of so many loving and caring family members and friends.

Mama lived with me until her final days. After she had to be hospitalized, she was discharged to a facility in Tennessee where she had briefly been in earlier years for rehab. Knowing Mama did not feel secure by herself, we did not want to leave her alone. For approximately five weeks, someone always stayed with her while she was there at the facility. Several of her children were there with her in her room on the day she died, which was a few weeks before her ninety-third birthday. I like to think she realized she was *never alone* and was *deeply loved*. I consider it *one of my life's greatest blessings* to have been holding her hand when she took her last breath and left this earthly life to be in her heavenly home with God.

After Mama died and Landon graduated and moved out, my circumstances had significantly changed. I found myself wondering, *What now?*

I had truly been blessed while living in Lexington. I had been able to share my home with my grandchildren, my mother, and others throughout the years. I had enjoyed many wonderful and rewarding experiences with family and some great friends. I had faced several challenges, and by the grace of God, I had endured. I had been fortunate to continue learning. I enjoyed many happy and fun times. And most importantly, I had found an inner peace and a closer relationship with God.

I had really liked living in Lexington and felt very blessed to have been able to live there for twenty years.

SEVENTEEN

The Move

After my mother died and Landon had graduated from the University of Kentucky and had moved out, the house seemed empty. I found myself feeling far away from family. All my children lived in other Kentucky towns, approximately two hours away. All my grandchildren by now were either in high school or college, had graduated from college, or had jobs.

I had family members in other towns who were facing some major challenges. I found myself trying to help and support them from a distance, which meant a lot of driving and being gone overnight. I had made many trips back and forth when called upon, trying to help when needed for several years, and I was wondering if being closer would be easier for me to provide more support for them.

I realized I didn't need all the room I had once enjoyed in my Lexington house, and as I had gotten older, it was getting harder and harder for me to take care of the house and the yard. Although in relatively good health, I found I had less energy and stamina than in previous years, and all the responsibility of caring for the house and yard was becoming more of a chore, rather than the pleasure it had previously been.

I started thinking seriously about downsizing and considering my options for the years to come while I was still healthy. I no longer needed all the space, or for that matter, all the things that I had accumulated over the years.

Some of the things in my possession had been purchased for the benefit of my mother and were no longer useful to me. There were closets full of toys, games, and other items that had been for my grandchildren. I also had many items I had kept for over forty years, from times when I had previously moved from a different house. Several of the boxes I had kept were of materials I had saved from my teaching days. I had never really gone through them or discarded anything, but I had continued to store them in a closet or in the garage, thinking I would go through them at a later date.

For twenty years, I had been busy making a new life. I had enjoyed living in Lexington in a wonderful neighborhood, with wonderful neighbors and friends. They were always so helpful and supportive when I was by myself or when Mama or one of the grandsons were living there. If I needed help, or if anything looked out of the ordinary at my house, I could count on them. When my garage door might still be open at nine o'clock at night, one of them would let me know. If I had a minor repair, my neighbor friend would fix it. If we had a snow such that it looked like I might not be able to get out, my neighbor, his wife, or one of their boys would shovel my driveway.

I had found a church family I liked in Lexington and had joined several clubs and organizations. I was enjoying spending time with friends, going places with them, and planning outings with them. I really liked living in Lexington, but my circumstances had now changed. I began to think that there might be other changes or hard choices I should make while I was still of sound body and mind.

I considered a lot of options, both around Lexington and in other places, and I finally decided that moving to Bowling Green, Kentucky, would be the best choice for me. I would be closer to all my *own* children, most of my grandchildren, and many of my extended family who lived in the Nashville area. This would be more of a central location for me. As we had gotten older and all had grown families, I had hoped to be able to spend more time with my brothers and sisters, and I would then be closer to them.

Many years before, I had graduated from Western Kentucky University and had actually lived in Bowling Green for a short time. I knew I would like it there. After all, I had always liked anywhere I had ever lived.

I had a difficult choice to make!

I decided to make the move to Bowling Green! It was mind-boggling to think of everything I needed to do. I needed to find a place in Bowling

Green, and I needed to go through everything I had stored in the garage, closets, drawers, and cabinets. It made me tired to think about it, but I had a goal of living in a new home in Bowling Green in six months.

In the fall of 2018, I went to Bowling Green, leased an apartment for six months, and planned on keeping my Lexington house until I found a place there. I hired a mover to take what I needed from my Lexington house to furnish the Bowling Green apartment, and I left the rest of my things in my Lexington house. I had planned on going through all my belongings before I moved. I started the process and gave many items to family members, friends, and charities, and I put much in the garbage.

During the six months I had the apartment in Bowling Green, I went back and forth from Lexington to Bowling Green. When I was staying in Bowling Green, I was driving around different neighborhoods and searching the real estate websites to look for a new place to live. When I was in Lexington, I was going through cabinets, drawers, and closets and separating my possessions, deciding which to keep, which to give away, and which to put in the trash. My good friend Ellie was always there to help me when I was in Lexington. I'm not sure I could have ever done the move if she had not been there to help me organize, clean, sort, and pack. She was amazing! She was such a help to me, and to this day, she remains one of my good friends!

After four months of going back and forth, looking at houses, apartments, and condos, I found a condo I really liked. I immediately thought it was perfect for me. It was practically ready for me to move in, as the owners had just remodeled and the husband had been transferred to Florida before they could actually enjoy it. There were only a few minor details that needed to be taken care of before I could move in.

As a temporary arrangement, I decided what items I needed to move from my Bowling Green apartment to my new condo and what I temporarily needed to move to my new condo from my Lexington house in order to be able to stay or work at either of the three places. I left the items at my Lexington house that my realtor advised should be kept there to prepare for putting the house on the market and showing the house to potential buyers. All the other things I wanted to keep were to be stored at a nice barn which belonged to my son and daughter-in-law. For a brief time, I was house poor!

I then had to clean and prepare my Lexington house to be ready to put on the market, leaving just the pieces of furniture and decor that my realtor thought should be kept there to make it show well. I went through all my belongings, left the furniture and decor in the Lexington house that the realtor suggested, and moved the rest. I then had everything ready to show the house.

I put my house on the market, and it sold within a week. I had thirty days to vacate the property. The movers came and cleared out the Lexington house, taking some things to Bowling Green to my new condo, moving items from my rented apartment in Bowling Green to my new condo, and dropping off the rest from both places to my son and daughter-in-law's barn. I finished the move into my new condo in March of 2019, a month before my six-month apartment lease expired.

For the next few months, my children and grandchildren were offered the opportunity to go to the barn and get anything they wanted or could use from the remainder of the things I was not going to use. I was happy that several of them took some nice things that I no longer needed or could fit into my condo. It made me happy to see some of the items in their own houses that I no longer needed or could use. After the kids and grandkids got what they wanted, we had a barn sale in the fall, and there were quite a few items left that were given to charity.

From when I had begun to plan the move, to going through all my possessions, driving back and forth between towns, dividing and moving the furniture, and disposing of unwanted or unneeded items—from beginning to end—the *entire* process of moving from Lexington to Bowling Green in 2019 took almost the entire year.

Bowling Green had grown and changed tremendously since I had previously gone to college at Western Kentucky University, or when I had previously lived there. I had to learn my way around in new and unfamiliar places. However, I was getting settled in and was very happy with my condo and my new surroundings. I was living in an established neighborhood with many nice houses, a nearby golf course, and well-maintained yards with nice landscaping.

I really began to like the simplicity of condo living, which I found to be great for me at this age and stage in my life. I no longer had to do my own yard work and outdoor maintenance. I paid a homeowner's association fee, but it was less than I had been paying in Lexington to hire others to help with what I could not do for myself anymore. I had no steps to go up and down in my new condo, which was a plus for me at my age. I was close to doctors and medical facilities, and a convenient distance from groceries and numerous wonderful places to eat. I was close to several entertainment venues. There were many educational opportunities in the college town of Bowling Green. There were several nearby churches to visit, one of which I hoped would soon become my new church home.

Moving was a hard choice! But it was one of my good choices!

I was very happy with my move!

EIGHTEEN

More Good Days to Come

The years of our life are 70, or even by reason of strength 80; yet their
span is but toil and trouble, they are soon gone and we fly away.
—Psalms 90:10, NIV

After getting settled in Bowling Green in the spring of 2019, at the age of
seventy-seven, I was feeling abundantly blessed. God had been faithful! All
throughout my life, He had provided for me abundantly. I had everything
materially that I needed. Compared to many of my friends and associates, I
had lived a long life. I was no longer dwelling on what could have been or
should have been. I was reading and studying the Bible more and trusting
more and more in God's truths. God had forgiven me, and I had forgiven
myself for past mistakes and failures, and I was trusting in His grace and
mercy as I tried to live closer to Him each day.

As I spent time getting acclimated to my new surroundings, I spent
many hours changing information on various personal accounts, and
finding new doctors, a new bank, new stores in which to make necessary
purchases, and new places to eat. The first few months were busy months.
Anything I needed was very conveniently located to where I had purchased
my new condo.

After taking care of many of the more immediate concerns, I began
to meet new neighbors and to make new friends in Bowling Green. I
started looking for a new home church. I looked around and visited
several churches for several weeks until I became drawn to Bowling Green
Christian Church, which was conveniently located to where I lived. I later

placed my membership there. I began to get involved in some ministries there, and I especially enjoyed my Sunday school class, which was led by an excellent teacher and where I enjoyed the fellowship of several wonderful, like-minded Christians. I had missed those interactions and discussions for quite some time.

It turned out that it is indeed a small world, as I crossed paths there at the church with several people I had known from years before. A few of them had actually been my former first-grade students. Several others were related to some of my former friends and associates. I had known some of their parents, or they had known some of my relatives. Those different connections, and the friendly people, helped me to soon feel at home at my new church.

In many ways, life in Bowling Green was becoming just as enjoyable as my earlier years in other places. I had met many wonderful people in each place I had lived throughout the years. I had enjoyed every city or town, met many new people, and made new friends, many of whom still remain friends today. I had always experienced periods of enjoyment as well as challenges to face wherever I lived. Some of the most difficult periods while living in each place had many *beautiful* days. There were always many reasons to be thankful, and I was again experiencing great thankfulness after moving back to Bowling Green.

I was no longer dealing with a relationship issue of my own, which might have clouded my thinking at various times throughout my life. In some instances, I felt my own relationship issues may have actually minimized the help and support I otherwise might have been able to give to my children, my grandchildren, or others in the past. I think it was harder when I was in a negative situation myself in prior years to effectively address some of the concerns of others. My hope was that I would now be better able to do that.

> With age comes wisdom, but sometimes age comes alone.
> —Oscar Wilde

In all truthfulness, I had spent many earlier years getting older *without learning much*, but all these years later, I was hopefully now a wiser person! I had realigned my priorities and was continuing to work on my spiritual life. I felt I was in a much better position— emotionally, spiritually, and financially—to help with some of the life challenges that might now be facing some of my children, grandchildren, and friends.

I was confident that I was now ready to try to more effectively do for others what I remembered from the words of the song "Why Me," which so many years ago helped me to start on *my own* renewed spiritual journey: "Maybe Lord, I can show someone else what I've been through myself on my way back to you."

About a year after I moved to Bowling Green, my older brother died (God rest his soul). This was a sad period for me, and quite naturally, it caused me to think more and more about my own mortality. I was the oldest sibling left in our family, and in the natural order of progression, I found myself thinking that I could be next to reach my final days.

I began more seriously thinking about whether I had all my affairs in order. I knew I was in a saved relationship with God, but I began to spend some time on practical tasks that I thought might need to be considered upon my passing. I wanted to try to make things go smoother for my children upon my passing.

For years, one thing I had often thought about and thought I might someday want to do was to write a book. (I originally had that thought over twenty years ago, after my third divorce.) As I experienced both highs and lows and had grown throughout my healing years, I had actually *written down* some of my thoughts. Some of these were in periods of sadness, and others in times of joy. Several of these were letters written to individuals in times of extreme displeasure, which were never mailed (and really just turned out to be good therapy for me).

Several months ago, while in the midst of a challenging, ongoing family concern, *the idea for this book resurfaced*. That was the day I saw the skunk in the middle of the road! That was a day when I had a *hard choice* to make, and a day when I figuratively just had to *run over the skunk*.

After that day, I began to look at many of the writings I had kept over the years, and I reread what I had been thinking at the time and how I had been feeling. I recounted some of my painful and difficult choices, and the consequences that followed when I had indeed figuratively run over the skunk. I was witnessing some of my family members going through difficult times, and I knew of others who had also experienced difficult times, some of whom were *even now* in the midst of making difficult choices of their own.

It was as if God was saying to me, *now is the time to tell your story!* So I began to write!

I wanted others to know that they were not alone in living through difficult experiences and making difficult choices.

I wanted to share some of my own life experiences and choices with the hope that, by doing so, the *faith, hope,* and *endurance* of others might be strengthened after difficult choices they, too, might have made or *will* make. I *especially* wanted my children and grandchildren to know more about my life, from the beginning to the present, and to see how, after almost eighty years, my *own* life had been shaped by my prior experiences and choices, both good and bad.

Through them all, I *learned* from them and became the person I am today, with the beliefs I have today. If my story is an encouragement to my children, my grandchildren, or even just *one other person*, it will be worthwhile.

Some of the hardest lessons I learned throughout my life were the ones my *spirit* needed the most. I'm sorry to say that I've probably broken every one of the Ten Commandments, either in my actions or in the thoughts and intentions of my heart. In my spiritual healing, I found that I especially needed to renew my mind and my thinking! Some of my inward *thoughts* and *feelings* were what I grew to believe had caused the most turmoil in my *spirit* and *soul*, and for so many years had kept me from experiencing the *peace* for which I had so desperately longed.

Today, with a renewed spirit and after much study and refinement of thinking, when I look back at my life, I believe that *most* of my problems and difficulties could be summed up in one word: PRIDE! From my early life, during my school years, and onward throughout the years with my relationships and interactions with others, I can now better see how pride—and everything that *one word* encompasses—had many times, and in many different ways, raised its angry head.

Pride is an attitude of the heart. It is a way of thinking. It is not like adultery, murder, lying, drunkenness, cheating, stealing, and other more visible sins, but it is just as destructive to our souls. Pride can be compared to the wind. It is true that we cannot see the wind, but we can see the *effects* of the wind.

The same is true with pride, and in my life, I have experienced some of the effects of a prideful heart.

Humility is the opposite of pride!

When I think of the difference between pride and humility, I'm reminded of a humorous old country song written by Mac Davis, the words of which actually reveal some prideful thoughts. (Not all necessarily thoughts I have had.)

"It's Hard to Be Humble"

O Lord it's hard to be humble
When you're perfect in every way.
I can't wait to look in the mirror
Cause I get better looking each day.

(That's just the first verse. There's more!)

By no means do I believe that I am *alone* in fighting the sin of pride and trying to become more humble! Pride led to the commencement of *all* sin. It goes back to the very beginning of time. It was pride which overthrew the devil, from whom arose the origin of sin. Afterward, it was what led Eve to eat the forbidden fruit when she did not follow God's plans and directions.

According to the Scriptures, many of us may even be *unaware* of our pridefulness!

> The pride of your heart has deceived you.
> —Obadiah 3:3 NIV

As I look back at many experiences and choices in my life, I believe that could describe me. As I made mistakes and have studied and grown in my spiritual life, my awareness has grown as to what it means to have a prideful heart. Some of my prior feelings, thoughts, or actions were reflective of this unawareness.

At times in the past, I had been guilty of doing whatever it took to make someone else happy, trying to get approval to ensure continuation of a relationship, and trying to please others no matter what. In trying to be a people pleaser, it was often to the detriment of trying to please God.

Paul wrote in Galatians 1:10 (NLT), "Obviously, I'm not trying to win the approval of people, but of God. If pleasing people were my goal, I would not be Christ's servant."

I felt like I deserved to be happy, to be loved and appreciated. Then when I experienced heartbreak, disappointment, and suffering, I became very frustrated and angry with others. I even *questioned God* whenever I thought I was trying to do the right thing and didn't think I *deserved* the difficulties and hardships that I was experiencing in my life.

In actuality, I *was not* really *entitled* to anything except punishment for my sins! Too many times, I was not resting in God's grace and mercy which was so readily available to me.

> For everyone has sinned, we all fall short of God's glorious standard.
> —Romans 3:23, NLT

> For the wages of sin is death, but the free gift of God
> is eternal life through Christ Jesus our Lord.
> —Romans 6:23, NLT

Many times in the past, I was an *ungrateful* person. With a proud and stubborn heart, I found myself complaining a lot, instead of being thankful and appreciative for all my many blessings. The world didn't revolve around me, even though at times I might have wished it would or acted like it should. I had a proud and ungrateful heart by not recognizing that God had already given me everything I *really* needed.

> Fear the Lord, you his godly people, for those who
> fear him will have all that they need.
> —Psalms 34:9 NLT

In many ways, I was a hypocrite! I thought I was not nearly as "bad" as many other people, which is the essence of having a *prideful spirit*. Finding fault with others, whether or not overtly stated, can translate into a holier-than-thou attitude. Although I went to church on a regular basis and may have had the appearance of being virtuous, I was sometimes blinded to my own prideful sins, even though they might not have been visible to others. It was a heart thing, if nothing else!

Note what harsh words Jesus had for hypocrites in Matthew 23:5–7 (NLT):

> "Everything they do is for show. On their arms they wear extra wide prayer boxes with scripture verses inside, and they wear robes with extra long tassels. And they love to sit at the head table at banquets and in the seats of honor in the synagogues. They love to receive respectful greetings as they walk in the marketplaces, and to be called Rabbi."

When becoming occupied with my own difficult circumstances and feeling like my life was out of control, I often became *fearful, worried,* and *anxious,* rather than having a strong, steadfast faith. The times when I strayed and *took my eyes off Jesus,* my situation usually worsened. I was not humbly resting in God's promises that He would be with me through it all!

> Immediately Jesus reached out His hand and caught him,
> "You of little faith!" he said, "Why did you doubt?"
> —Matthew 14:31, NIV

I often lived as if I was capable enough and smart enough to solve my problems myself and find a way on my own to be happy. It was as if I didn't need anyone else to tell me what to do! Some of my thoughts, words, and actions were contrary to God's will, instead of trying to follow His Word in all situations. In essence, I was *rebelling against God,* saying, "I knew better than God," just as Adam and Eve did in the beginning.

Pride deceives us into thinking we can *do life* on our own, that we are capable, independent, unstoppable, and self-reliant. It's as if we think we don't need God! We think we don't need His help, grace, mercy, courage, and hope. With a *humble heart,* we submit ourselves to God in prayer because we know we can do nothing without Him, so we talk to Him more!

Praying more became a very important help to me in having a brighter and more peaceful life, and *today* I need to continue to pray even more!

God doesn't want me to come to Him in prayer *only* in times of trouble. He wants to hear my thanks, my prayers of gratitude for all He has given me and all He has done for me.

As I have gotten older, I have become a much more thankful person than in years past. I know that everything I *am* and everything I *have* comes from God, the giver of all good things!

Don't worry about anything, instead pray about everything. Tell God what you need, and thank Him for all He has done. Then you will experience God's peace which exceeds anything we can understand. His peace will guard your hearts and minds as you live in Christ Jesus.
—Philippians 4:6–7 NLT

In the coming days, I want to become more *humble* and less *prideful.* My prayer is that I will continue to be transformed daily by the Holy Spirit in the struggle with pride in my life.

Many times throughout the years, I have been humbled by some of my choices and experiences! But I no longer want to be held hostage to my past, whether years ago, months ago, or even days ago. God is faithful! God forgives His children! Instead of holding on to wrongdoings, He wants His children to let go as well!

He does not treat us as our sins deserve or repay us according to our iniquities, for as high as the heavens are above the earth, so great is his love for those who fear Him, as far as the east is from the west, so far has He removed our transgressions from us.
—Psalms 103:10–12, NIV

Since God, by His love and grace, has forgiven me of so much, in order to be right with God, I know I have to be forgiving of those who I feel have mistreated or wronged me. I need to forgive them, just as God has forgiven me. The rest is up to God!

For if ye forgive men their trespasses, your heavenly father will also forgive you; but if ye forgive not men their trespasses, neither will your Father forgive your trespasses.
—Matthew 6:14–15, KJV

As we read in the book of Matthew, we will be judged by the same standards by which we judge others. Matthew 7:1-2 NIV "Do not judge, or you too will be judged. For in the same way you judge others, you will be judged, and with the measure you use, it will be measured to you."

It is very sobering to think that, if we judge someone harshly when they do wrong, God will also harshly judge us when we do wrong. Whatever measure or standard we use to judge others, God will also use with us. Judging, payback for being wronged or getting revenge are all best left to God.

I will take revenge; I will pay them back. In due time, their feet will slip,
their day of disaster will arrive and their destiny will overtake them.
—Deuteronomy 32:35–36, NLT

In a *humble* manner, I want to continually recommit to these scriptural truths. Instead of harshly judging or trying to get even with those who I feel have wronged me, or might wrong me in the future, I need to be loving and forgiving toward others, and let God take care of the rest!

I know I will continue to have challenges ahead. If I see a family member or friend hurting or suffering in any way, it will be my tendency to want to help them, maybe even to try to "fix" them. I hope never to be so uncaring as to do the easy thing and think or say to any of them who might be having a problem or going through a difficult time- just get over it! Instead, I would want to try to the best of my ability to help them get through it!

One hard truth I have learned is that I *cannot* "fix" others. I'm not smart enough! I don't know all the answers! I don't understand everything, and I don't have to! I'm not God! As hard as I sometimes in the past might have tried to make others do what I thought was right, I learned I could not "fix" them any more than they could "fix" me.

I might be able to help others *discern good from evil*, or point others to scriptural truths, but I cannot read minds and know what is in a person's heart. I need to be humble enough to realize that I am not all-knowing!

Those whom I *think* might need "fixing," or those whom I might want to "fix" or want others to "fix," might not need "fixing" nearly as much as I need to work on my *own* shortcomings. My sins might not be visible to others, and instead of trying to "fix" others, I might actually need a "heart transplant" of my own!

> Hypocrite! First get rid of the log in your own eye; then you will
> see well enough to deal with the speck in your friend's eye.
> —Matthew 7:5, NLT

Even though my life has been far from perfect, and I strayed from God's Word many times, I am thankful that He did not give up on me! He *did* allow me to suffer at times, but enduring through these times only helped me to draw closer to Him.

Today I see some of my own children, grandchildren, relatives, friends, and others who are also suffering at times. I pray that, as children of God, they will know that God loves them dearly, and that He can use their most difficult periods of life to help them draw closer to Him, just as He did with me!

Happiness, for me, has *not* been about getting all I thought I wanted in life, but about learning to enjoy and be thankful for all my God-given blessings!

A grateful person is a happy person!

> Happy is that people whose God is the Lord.
> —Psalms 144:15 KJV

I am now almost eighty years old, and I am a mother, grandmother, and great-grandmother. I have always felt a deep sense of responsibility for those I helped bring into this world. I want them to know I will always be there for them to help in any way I possibly can. Whether they seek my help, ask for my advice, or listen to my counsel is then up to them. My sincere desire and prayer is to see them functioning as godly, happy people before God calls me to leave this earth.

As long as I have the strength and ability, I will continue to try to teach and help my family, as well as others by word and by example. I will continue to pray for wisdom, and that God will use me in some small way to be a blessing to others. At my age and stage in life, it may be as simple as showing His love by a kind or thoughtful deed, with a kind or encouraging word, or maybe even through this book!

I hope to continue learning, growing, and being renewed daily by the Holy Spirit as I continue to live in Bowling Green. I want to continue to try to be a godly example to my family, my extended family, and my friends. I want to show grace, mercy, kindness, and love to each and every person I meet. I want to be the best representative of Christ that I can possibly be while I am still here on God's beautiful earth.

I do not know how many days, months, or years this Big Clifty farm girl may have left. I *do* know life is to be treasured! Each day becomes more precious as we get older, have to slow down, and realize that our days are numbered. I hope to spend the remainder of mine, inasmuch as is possible, with those I love. Not everyone is given the chance to grow old, so I want to appreciate and thank God for every single day He gives me yet to live.

There will always be much love and a special place in my heart for my three sons, my seven grandchildren, and my three great-grandchildren (and any yet to come). Those who love the ones I love are also very special to me! Each and every day becomes more precious with them as I live on. I hope whatever help or encouragement I might have been to them, might continue to be so to them, or that the love I have shown to them, will be paid forward to others throughout each of their own lives.

My prayer for them, as well as for any other reader, is that someday we will all be together and praising our God in a better and perfect world!

ACKNOWLEDGMENTS

In remembrance of my loving parents and older brother who are now deceased!

Thanks be to God for a long-lived life!

To all my siblings and their spouses, thank you for your love, support, and encouragement as I began and continued my eighty-year story, of which you are an important part. Thank you to my friends and others who loved and supported me at different stages of my life. A special thanks to Jesse, my brother-in-law, who helped with technical and computer-related concerns as I began to formulate my ideas and has continued to help along the way as I completed this book. I love and appreciate you all!

Printed in the United States
by Baker & Taylor Publisher Services